REDISCOVER THE JOYS AND BEAUTY OF NATURE WITH TOM BROWN, JR.

THE TRACKER
Tom Brown's classic true story—the most powerful and magical high-spiritual adventure since *The Teachings of Don Juan*

THE SEARCH
The continuing story of *The Tracker*, exploring the ancient art of the new survival

THE VISION
Tom Brown's profound, personal journey into an ancient mystical experience, the Vision Quest

THE QUEST
The acclaimed outdoorsman shows how we can save our planet

THE JOURNEY
A message of hope and harmony for our earth and our spirits—Tom Brown's vision for healing our world

GRANDFATHER
The incredible true story of a remarkable Native American and his lifelong search for peace and truth in nature

AWAKENING SPIRITS
For the first time, Tom Brown shares the unique mediation exercises used by students of his personal Tracker Classes

THE WAY OF THE SCOUT
Tom Brown's real-life apprenticeship in the ways of the scouts—ancient teachings as timeless as nature itself

THE SCIENCE AND THE ART OF TRACKING
Tom Brown shares the wisdom of generations of animal trackers—revelations that awaken us to our own place in nature and in the world

AND THE BESTSELLING SERIES OF TOM BROWN'S FIELD GUIDES

ABOUT THE AUTHOR

At the age of eight, Tom Brown, Jr., began to learn tracking and hunting from Stalking Wolf, a displaced Apache Indian. Today Brown is an experienced woodsman whose extraordinary skill has saved many lives, including his own. He manages and teaches one of the largest wilderness and survival schools in the U.S. and has instructed many law enforcement agencies and rescue teams.

THE SCIENCE AND ART OF TRACKING

Tom Brown, Jr.

Photos by Debbie Brown

Illustrations by Nancy Klein

BERKLEY BOOKS, NEW YORK

This book is an original publication of The Berkley Publishing Group.

THE SCIENCE AND ART OF TRACKING

A Berkley Book / published by arrangement with
the author

PRINTING HISTORY
Berkley trade paperback edition / February 1999

ISBN: 0-425-15772-5

BERKLEY®
Berkley Books are published by The Berkley Publishing Group,
a division of Penguin Group (USA) Inc.,
375 Hudson Street, New York, New York 10014.
BERKLEY and the "B" design
are trademarks belonging to Penguin Group (USA) Inc.

PRINTED IN THE UNITED STATES OF AMERICA

20   19   18   17   16   15   14   13

DEDICATION

It all began with a track, a track that reached back into another time, a distant time, the time of life's dawning. This ancient track, found lying on what was once the primordial shore, wrapped in the medium we call a fossil and Grandfather called a "talking stone," brought Grandfather and me together. This stone and this young boy were his Vision, and his Vision became mine. It was through the mystery of the tracks that I learned his way. The way of the Earth and of "oneness."

The tracks have always been a major part of my life. Long before my school opened its doors, long before I became a writer, and long before I was known for the teaching of survival, awareness, and philosophy, there was the track. I became known as the Tracker, tracking the lost and the criminal, assisting, then disappearing back into the isolation of the wilderness. It was the tracks that began my school, my writing, and the fulfillment of my Vision.

The tracks then are my life, for it is the tracks that have always guided my life. This book then is my legacy—Grandfather's legacy—of the spirit of tracking . . . and it will remain the most important physical work of my life.

It is with the importance of this Vision in mind that I dedicate this book, with all of my love, to my wife, Debbie, and our sons, Coty Tracker Brown and River Scout Brown—who taught me to read and follow new tracks, the tracks of love, the tracks of the heart.

AND SPECIAL THANKS

To my wife, Debbie, who pulled me from the bowels of despair. Who stood by me and guided me back to my Vision when I was ready to give it all up. Who gave me life and hope again, refocused my Vision, and has worked tirelessly behind the scenes to build the Tracker School so that our message will reach more people. Grandfather's Vision, my Vision, now has become her Vision and she has become my Vision.

To my son Coty, who loses his dad so often to the school and to the writing of books. His love remains unconditional, for deep in his little heart he knows the importance of the Vision. It is in him that I so often see Grandfather.

To my son Tommy, who for many years has given up his dad for the greater Vision, now compounded by the additional separation of time and distance. Yet I also find love and understanding.

To my mom, my dad, and my brother, Jim, who have had to put up with me all these years, but who've still allowed me to follow my heart.

To my greater family, the Horrocks, Debbie's family—Bill, Linda, Billy, Michael, Chris, Uncle Bill, and all their kids, who accepted me and love me despite my Visionary moodiness and quirks.

To Nana, who has become like a real grandmother to me. I want to thank her for her wisdom and love, and for a good swift boot in the pants when I need it most. Nana, I love you.

And to all of my instructors at the Tracker School, past and present, and to all of my students, who make this Vision a living reality. I thank you all. For it is through all of you, the greater family, that this book has become possible.

Last, but not least, a sincere thanks to my editors, John Talbot and Tom Colgan, who saw me through the impossibilities of writing this book and putting my heart to words.

CONTENTS

FOREWORD
by Debbie Brown

The art of tracking has always been associated with mystical native people who would begin at a very young age and continue perfecting their skill throughout their lives. Many of us spontaneously try tracking when we see crystal clear footprints in sand or mud. But if that animal or human goes into a leaf-covered area or onto debris-rich ground cover, we immediately stop trying, assuming the trail is lost. Tracking means following footprints through any terrain, including across a linoleum or wood floor, or on a road, or over exposed bedrock.

My husband, Tom Brown, Jr., is known as "the Tracker" because of his ability to follow footprints across any terrain. He is not a Native American but, as the tradition dictates, he did start learning the art of tracking at a very young age. He still does tracking, himself, and he teaches everyday people to track quite easily in one week. His school, Tom Brown's Tracking, Nature, and Wilderness Survival School, in Asbury, New Jersey, brings people from all over the world to learn the ancient art.

It's amazing how much tracks influence our environment, yet no one even notices. Many mountains are the tracks left by moving glaciers, and an ant leaves a mark on the ground when gathering food. In between those two extremes there are tracks everywhere. All the bumps, curves, ridges, valleys, peaks, and bulges right under our feet were made by something.

They are not always made by the foot of an animal. The wind leaves a track on a bent-over tree, different marks are left by rain, sunshine, frosts, arid conditions, and so on. Every mound, hill, and crevice has something to teach us. The art of tracking is not merely the following of footprints in the ground, it is the all-encompassing ability to be aware and to understand why the landscape is the way it is.

In order to track, weather conditions, time of day, lay of the landscape, and state of mind all have to be considered. Awareness is the biggest factor, because without it a person is able to follow only the most obvious footprints in mud or sand.

Awareness in this case means knowing the environment, not just being alert when you're in the wilderness. Where do the animals lie down? sleep? eat? When do they eat? What do they like best? What do animals pay attention to and what do they ignore? These and many other questions are just the beginning of awareness. Think for a minute of every sense that a human body has: sight, smell, taste, hearing, touch, and intuition. All these

ingredients are part of awareness. In tracking, the ability to be highly aware
will be a great aid in finding the final track.

Tracking is used for many things: getting food when you're hungry,
finding lost people, and retracing the life of an animal. Tom can do all of
these things but it did not come easily. He spent ten years under the guid-
ance of Stalking Wolf, an Apache elder, whom Tom called Grandfather.
Grandfather had one mission, or Vision, in life—to teach someone everything he knew of the native peoples of North and South America. He
searched for sixty years before he found one person who would listen and
learn. In his travels he came across many people who were very interested
in what he had to teach, but none stayed with him long enough for him to
pass along the volumes of information he possessed. This mission was very
important to Grandfather. If the information he had was never taught, all
the knowledge of his people would be lost forever. Enter Tom.

At the young age of seven, Tom met Grandfather. The two of them
spent every possible moment after school, on weekends, and during holidays
together. It all started with a desire to knap an arrowhead. Tom learned
how to knap an arrowhead first out of glass, then chirt, then obsidian, then
stone, then quartzite. Then he learned how to make bone arrowheads. He
also learned the use of each different arrowhead. Grandfather made him
master each before he could start learning another. Over and over he tried
until a given type of arrowhead was beautiful and correctly done. Until then
there would be no more teaching. As the years went by, Grandfather's
teaching did not change; Tom always had to master the skill he was working
on before he went on to the next. And so it was with each and every skill.
Painfully at first, he would learn every aspect of a skill until he could do it
in any weather situation and under any circumstances. Tom fulfilled Grandfather's Vision, and Grandfather started Tom on the path he walks today.

Of all the skills Tom learned, tracking is his favorite. Tom always speaks
of "dirt time," the act of getting on your knees and studying a track for
hours at a time. Thousands of hours of "dirt time" were required for Tom
to learn to answer questions Grandfather awakened him to: What sex was
the animal? Did it have any injuries? How heavy was it? What time of day
did it pass? Was it nervous? What was its state of mind? Was it hungry?
Had it just eaten? Where was it headed? Was it in a rush to get there?
These and countless other questions needed to be answered.

Many little boys dream of meeting a Native American who would teach
them how to hunt with a bow and arrow. But none of those little boys was
Tom. There is something in Tom, an obsession, if you will, that drove him

to learn the skills. He had a passion to learn, an unstoppable yearning to discover the ancient ways and bring them to you and me. He wanted to unlock all the mysteries of the spiritual world.

Today, Tom spends every other week teaching, in hopes that sharing what he has learned will stop the abuse and rape of our Earth Mother. Too many people are destroying the place we all depend upon. The careless dumping of garbage, the extinction of animals, the rampant development of wilderness—all this weighs heavy on our minds. In every class that comes through, he wishes that each person will go out and tell others to stop what they are doing and understand the Earth beneath us. See the miracles that happen every day. Watch the sunrise and give thanks. Life in society today consists of an hour's drive to a job you hate; an hour's drive home; two minutes with the kids before they go to sleep; dinner, bed, and then do it all over again. Just so we can have one more VCR than the next door neighbor. Unfortunately, many people wait until they are sixty-five before they ask, "Is there more to life?"

There is more, and Tom can open the door for you to see it. What's silly is that it's so easy and it's right there under your nose.

Tom Brown, Jr., can give meaning to your life. He can teach you how to love each other; how to respect our home, the Earth; and the reason we are alive. Most of all, he can teach you how to live free from the bonds of society. You don't need it. He can also teach you to heal the sick or to find a medicinal plant, how to prepare it and what it is used for. The Native Americans knew how to use medicinal plants—and it was not a trial and error process. Tom also teaches tapping into the spiritual realm, which guides us and helps us understand life. The spiritual realm has always been the way of the Native Americans. It told them when to migrate, where to find food, what water is safe to drink, and how to live in accordance with the laws of nature. The laws of nature were the only laws, and if you did not obey them then you would not survive. Thus, the only way to absolutely know that a medicinal plant would cure your stomach ulcer, for example, was from some other source, a spiritual source. If you believe in yourself, and believe what you feel is the truth, then nature will take care of you.

My husband shows people how to tap into the world of the unseen and eternal. Many consider him a shaman in his ability to heal, or to know what's bothering you and to take care of it. However, if there is one term he does not like to apply to himself it is shaman. Although he possesses the abilities, he only considers himself a signpost, and a tattered one at that. His finger points the way for you. He wishes that no one follows him, for the jagged edge has made him bleed very deeply. Above all he is a human and shares all human distraction and temptation and falls victim as easily as anyone can. This path he chose comes with many sacrifices, pain, and loss. His deep desire to save our Earth drains the life from him. Yet he goes on, even as those who doubt him would see him fall; he still tries to reeducate one more person because that one person may be the one to change everything.

If you should see his face on the TV, teaching the skills of primitive man, keep in mind that he is working very hard for people. How can we live in a world without animals, trees, or drinking water?

THE SCIENCE
AND
ART OF TRACKING

INTRODUCTION

I grew up on the outer edge of a vast wilderness area called the Pine Barrens. Back then the pines came right to the edge of the river, the backwoods were still pristine, some people, called "Pineys," still lived off the land, and the forests remained relatively untraveled. As a child I had but two choices for recreation: to head to the distant town where most other kids hung out or to take to the forests. I chose the latter, for even when I was as young as five, my folks noticed that I preferred playing in the woods over any toy or sport society could provide. In fact, they have said that my passion for wild places and exploration transcended all other childhood endeavors. From my earliest recollections I remember my parents reading to me from nature books or books on Native American people; they said that I had no interest in any other subject.

I can vividly recall playing "Indian," as I used to call it, pretending the forest around my house was my real home. Yet I longed to learn more than just the superficial information that books could provide. I wanted more. I wanted to know how to survive, how to track, how to be aware, and, most of all, how to be an "Indian." My folks once told me that on my Christmas list when I was five years old the only item I requested was a book on how to live in the woods with nothing. Just like the Native Americans did. I was constantly bringing home flowers, leaves, dead animals, rocks, and all manner of things—especially questions. I begged my parents to tell me what these strange things were or to find a book that could.

Unfortunately, my folks could not afford to buy these books, and our local library's limited collection of nature books were of little local value. By the time I was six, according to my folks, when I prayed before going to bed at night, I always prayed for a teacher to teach me the ways of the woods. Someone who could unravel the many mysteries that I wanted answers for. My father, who had been an avid camper in Scotland, knew little of the local plants and animals. My only other teacher was my uncle Howard, who was a biologist, but his knowledge was very limited. He knew much about the function of things, which was fascinating, but little about the names of things. Less still about survival, tracking, and being an "Indian."

Certainly most kids loved to play cowboy, Indian, or soldier, but I did not want to play it, I wanted to live it. There were also very few other children around and their interests were far different from mine. In fact, I considered their interests rather boring. I became my own best friend and

1

had no problem entertaining myself to a point of complete absorption. I could spend hours watching ants, never growing tired or bored, always filled with wonder. Yet with all that I did, all that I tried to learn and observe, there was a deep frustration growing in me. I knew by heart every book about nature and Native Americans that my parents read to me. I prayed often in desperation. Yet I never let the frustration dampen my passion for wilderness exploration. Even though "my wilderness" was marked off by an invisible backyard fence that my dad erected in my mind, it still held me in constant awe.

That back fence, which didn't exist except in my mind, became the focus of a game. I asked my folks to extend the barriers every year at my birthday, for good grades in school, or for chores completed, and grandest were the times that my mom or dad would take me far out for a walk. As I grew older my collecting habits became more and more bizarre. My kindergarten career must still be talked about by Mrs. Murry to this day, if she is still living. She came to loathe Show-and-Tell. When other kids were bringing in dolls, models, and other toys, I brought in my treasures from nature. I loved showing the class these things, retelling of their collection or capture in vivid detail. At first I had brought in plants and rocks. My skull collection was met with apprehension. It came to a climax with a snake and finally a dead and rather odiferous skunk, of which I was exceptionally proud. The day of the skunk marked the end of my participation in Show-and-Tell—only two months into the year at that.

My reputation must have preceded me, for when Show-and-Tell began in the first grade, I was barred from participating with anything found outside. I then became probably the first environmentalist in my town. I brought in old cans, paper, empty oil cans, and other seemingly useless discards of people. I told the class what these things did to "my woods," as I called them. The students showed mild disinterest, of course, but my teacher, Mrs. Thompson, was amazed. I found out that she was an avid animal and plant lover as well as bird-watcher. She told my parents that she was amazed at my sensitivity, especially at the ripe old age of six. When she showed up at my house one evening after school I knew I was probably in deep trouble, especially with that scary word, *sensitivity*, that she used. Imagine my amazement when my folks hugged me after she left.

Then one day, just a few months after my seventh birthday, I met Stalking Wolf, and my world changed forever. Stalking Wolf was the grandfather of my "bestest" friend, Rick. Rick shared my interest and passion for nature. Looking back now I don't think it took but ten minutes for us to become best friends, for no one else that I knew shared my interest in the wild things. I did not recognize his heritage that first day. Not until he introduced me to his grandfather, Stalking Wolf, an Apache elder. When I saw Grandfather I thought I was dreaming. His dress, his mannerisms, and everything about him exuded intense and limitless knowledge. He was spry and alert, especially for eighty-three years old. To me he was the spirit of the wilderness and possessed all the knowledge I could ever hope for.

Although he ended up staying more than ten years, Grandfather, as both Rick and I called Stalking Wolf, had originally come to our town to visit only for a month. The friction between his son and him was intense. His son, Rick's father, hated the Native Americans. Being a half-breed back in the '50s was, in his eyes, the lowest of humiliations, especially considering the state of reservation life back then. Joining the Navy was his way of putting his heritage behind him. Neither Rick nor I could understand this way of thinking. Rick's mother and his brother loved Grandfather, but Rick's father barely tolerated him, and any time they spoke it was in the harshest tones. Yet Grandfather would always be so kind and loving to Rick.

Rick's father tried to keep Rick out of the woods as much as he could, yet Rick would always find a way to go out with Grandfather and me every day. I was eventually disliked by Rick's dad too. I was looked upon as a "dumb hick" who had a bad influence on his son, especially given my devotion and allegiance toward Grandfather. Yet we managed, never fully understanding the hatred, at least not until we got much older. Even today any prejudice is beyond my understanding. As Grandfather once said, "When we can stop categorizing people as white, black, red, Protestant, Jew, man, or woman, and just see people, then truly we will have become civilized."

Grandfather's knowledge was astounding and even now, as I look back, it seems to have been limitless. We could count on several things with Grandfather's teachings. The first was that he was a "Coyote teacher"; second, he demanded hard work and passion for what was taught; third, we had to show an impassioned need for what he taught; and fourth, he would not teach us anything new unless we had mastered the old. He also expected us to practice the old skills every day. A Coyote teacher is rare indeed in our society, for a Coyote teacher makes you work for the knowledge you obtain. Questions are not answered in a straightforward way but rather a direction is pointed out, or another question is asked in order to make us search for answers. We had to supply the passion, the intense need to know, and the long and grueling practice time needed to perfect the skills.

Yet one of the things I most vividly remember about the way Grand-father taught skills is that they were always accompanied with a parable, or a story, or even a spiritual concept related to the skill. By far my favorite stories were those of the Scouts. To me, the Scouts were the deities of wilderness. I am not talking about the so-called scouts who led the army to track and round up Geronomo. The Scouts Grandfather referred to were of a secret Medicine Society within the tribal structure. They were simply the best. They could survive easily in the most hostile wilderness, wilderness that would kill most anyone else. They were the most aware of the tribe, for they were the eyes and ears of their people. Leading them to the best hunting, gathering, and camping grounds. Keeping the tribe away from dan-ger. Most of all, they were the best trackers. The best in the universe, as far as I was concerned. To date, I have never met or even heard of anyone who comes close.

The stories of the Scouts became my model for living. These were the best of the best. They were masters of wilderness, who lived in total har-mony with the land. They moved as the shadows, mastering camouflage and stalking to a point of invisibility. They could get right into the middle of an enemy encampment without being observed. They could read the symphony of movement and sound around them and know what was going on many miles away. Most of all they could glance at a track and read into the maker's very soul. To them the track was not only a window to the past, an intimate view of the animal or man who made it, but also a means of keeping them-selves and their tribe safe. Tracking was their doorway to the universe, where they could know all things through the tracks.

Beyond the fact that the Scouts could track across solid rock with ease, their knowledge of tracking went far beyond even the wildest possibilities. The Scouts refined tracking to an intense science and art. They saw a track as more than just a lifeless depression in the ground that told little more than the time of passage, the kind of being who made it, and its weight. Inside each track they saw an infinite miniature landscape. Hills, valleys, ridges, peaks, domes, and pocks within these tracks were not unlike the larger geological features found on the grand landscapes and vistas around them. Thus, each feature inside the track was identified and named, usually after the larger geological features found upon the grander landscapes. Each of these track features was caused by a distinct movement, external or in-ternal, by the maker of the track. I call these miniature landscape features *pressure releases,* and the Scouts identified well over five thousand of them.

This is not the work of just one Scout, for no one could amass this much information and detail in a lifetime. Not in several lifetimes. These pressure releases are an accumulation of countless generations of knowledge. And it is the science and art of pressure releases that is the subject of this book. There are only two elders I know of still living who possess the wisdom of the pressure releases. Both are past one hundred years old now. In all the tracking cases I have been on throughout the world I have never met anyone who even had a clue as to the function of these pressure releases, far less seen them. Thus if you have ever heard the term *pressure release* or any of the information contained in this book, then you can safely assume that it was taught by me, passed on by Grandfather, and originated by a vast lineage of Scouts. Even from the onset of his teachings, Grandfather demanded that I learn the pressure releases exactly, for I would be the only one who then possessed the wisdom. I would then have to pass it on to future generations.

My Tracking, Nature, and Wilderness Survival School is now over twenty years old. Part of my ambition during the past twenty years has been to pass on the knowledge of the pressure releases. I feared that if anything ever happened to me this knowledge, and many other skills, would be dead. To further ensure that this knowledge lives on I decided to write this book, so that those I will never meet can still share its power. However, these pressure releases are not mine. They belong to Grandfather and the many Scouts who came before him. I am just doing for you what Grandfather did for me. I am giving you the tools that will open a world of tracking beyond your wildest dreams and expectations. And thus keeping alive information that would be lost forever.

1. TRACKING AND AWARENESS

Grandfather did not and could not separate the concepts of tracking and awareness. To him, they were both part of the same consciousness. One could not exist or be whole without the other. Awareness without tracking became a shallow experience, where no understanding of the psyche of animals could be achieved nor, for that matter, could the entire fabric of nature be comprehended. In fact, the awareness of animals and the life forces of nature would be forever out of reach as well as incomprehensible. Tracking without awareness makes a prison of the trail, where nothing exists outside the trail itself.

The simplest understanding of how tracking enhances and broadens awareness can be found in the concept of "sign" tracking. Sign tracking involves finding the elements of a landscape that, when combined, make up the foundation for abundant animal life. These elements are: a rich variety of vegetation, the availability of thick cover so that an animal feels secure that it can escape its enemies and raise its young, and finally, but not always necessarily, the presence of water. Though many animals obtain their water from succulent or dew-soaked browse, the presence of flowing or standing water will create a teeming biome.

These attributes combined create a tremendous area for herbivore life, and where there are herbivores, there are sure to be carnivores. These animal-rich areas are also marked by the various roadways that are worn into the landscape. The trails, runs, pushdowns, beds, lays, feeding areas, watering areas, escape routes, and hides all make up the "signs" found throughout these animal biomes. (See *Tom Brown's Field Guide to Nature Observation and Tracking* for detailed information on sign tracking.) Not all parts of a landscape contain these life-sustaining features.

Grandfather once said, "I've seen people looking for deer in the middle of the ocean." What he was saying is that unless a person knows how to read landscapes through the eyes of a tracker then he has as much chance of seeing wildlife as looking for deer in the ocean. Not all parts of a landscape are rich in wildlife. Some areas are better than others and it is best to look at the land like islands in the sea. It is on the islands that the largest concentration and variety of wildlife will be found, not in the oceans between. Observe for a moment the elements of a deep forest. A deep forest has poor ground cover due to the upper canopy of treetops blocking out the sun. And poor ground cover means very little diversity in the vegetation and very little cover. So too the middle of a field may contain a great diversity of vegetation but very little cover. That is not to say that these areas do not have wildlife, but that wildlife is very limited both in population size and in number of species.

What we are looking for is the kind of landscape that sits between forest and field, or between waterways and fields. These are the fringe areas, the "islands" of animal life, which contain all of the elements that support a vast assortment of animals. This "landscape" tracking, as Grandfather called it, gives the observer the edge and directs him to where the animals will be found. This one simple aspect of tracking expands the basic awareness level and makes excursions into the wild more productive. Tracking thus first teaches us to observe the landscape as a whole, then directs us to where the greatest animal populations are to be found. Without this basic knowledge of landscapes and "sign," our travels will be blessed with very few animal sightings.

When we track an animal, we learn much about its life. Each track becomes a word and each trail a sentence, a paragraph, or a chapter of an animal's life. We know what it eats, where it sleeps, where it hides, and when it drinks water. We know what it reacts to and what it ignores. We know its likes and dislikes, its interactions with other animals, and the very landscape it lives in and travels through. An animal is an instrument played by the landscape, and its sweet concerto defines both its species and its individuality. Simply stated, the more that we know about a particular species of animal, the better we will see it physically and spiritually. It is this knowledge—a practical knowledge, not found in the dusty mechanics of a field guide, but in the reality of the living track—that creates an intimacy and understanding of the animal.

I remember how frustrated I was during the first few months I was with Grandfather. Rick and I would explore for the better part of a day and find one or two deer, possibly a lone fox or weasel, and on rare occasions a turkey or mink. Grandfather would sit in one place and within an hour point out a dozen deer, half as many foxes, countless weasels, skunks, minks, opossums, raccoons, turkeys, hawks, owls, and innumerable birds, insects, and reptiles. At first we never ventured to ask him how he could accomplish such awareness. Granted, much of his awareness was at a spiritual level, but equally as much was in how he observed the landscape. It wasn't until our exasperation and frustration became unbearable that we finally asked him his secret.

Rick, Grandfather, and I had been hiking for much of the morning, heading to a distant camp. As was typical on such travels, each of us would point out to the others what animals we saw. On that particular morning, Rick had spotted two deer, Grandfather had spotted so many that I lost count, and I had spotted not a one. As we neared our camp I finally could take no more and flew into a rage. I knew that Rick's two deer had been dumb luck, but Grandfather's sightings had transcended all luck and probability. I was beyond frustration and I didn't hesitate to tell Grandfather so. My anger was only overshadowed by my embarrassment over having seen nothing. Rick's attitude was not much consolation, as he stood by, smirking at his success, quietly rubbing my failure in my face.

I asked Grandfather how he could see so many deer while we saw nothing. I even suggested that he had some kind of superhuman vision and hearing. He just giggled and said, "Your problem is not that you are watching the land in the wrong way, but that you do not know what land to watch. You do not know where to look and when you do look you look in the wrong place." That statement startled me because I had always assumed, as most people do, that animals could be found anywhere equally upon the landscape. That then became the day that Grandfather first combined awareness with tracking. He taught us how to read the "sign" and to see the islands on the landscape. That too was the first day I saw more than ten deer in an hour; the hour after Grandfather taught us how and where to look.

As my knowledge of tracking grew I soon discovered that not only do plants influence the animals, dictating what will live in a given area, but so too do the animals have a tremendous impact on plants. Each depends on and influences the other. So, not only is an animal an instrument played by the landscape, but the landscape is an instrument played by the animal. Thus the spheres of animal, plant, and land come together to form a whole. This whole is nature's fabric of consciousness, where each being, each element, each entity is a thread that makes up this grand tapestry of life. That tapestry cannot be whole if one thread is missing. Tracking brought us face-to-face with the spirit-that-moves-through-all-things and the dimensions beyond.

To be aware is to understand the interwoven fabric of life, and, to understand an individual fiber, we may explore it through a track. It is then the track that expands the awareness, but so too the awareness expands the track, where all becomes one. When we pour ourselves into the track, part of us becomes that track, and we become the whole. Our tracks, like all tracks, move within the realm of creation, but so too does the realm of creation move within our tracks. There is no inner or outer dimension, no separation of self, just that which Grandfather called "oneness." To understand the track is to understand the animal and its relationship to the land. It is also to understand our own place in the natural world.

Yet, to understand the oneness, the fabric of life, through tracking is to comprehend more than each individual strand. The fiber cannot stand alone, isolated and removed from the whole. Instead, each strand affects every other one and the whole. Each track is not isolated, or merely part of an overall trail. Each track reflects and records the world about it. A track becomes a story of action and reaction to the land and animals around it. Each grand and small nuance of movement is directed not only by the animal but also by the entirety of creation. It is in essence the center of a series of concentric rings of action, combined with countless other concentric rings to bring about a bigger picture of the past, recorded in each track.

The track shows a fox hesitating, pausing in trembling curiosity mixed with apprehension. It indicates a glance high and to the left. The track's concentric rings then beg the tracker's eyes to follow the gaze of the fox to a high branch. There he finds the defined puncture and scrape marks of an owl's talons. The fox track points to the owl's talon marks, and the talon marks lead to a flight to the ground, the death of a mouse, and the reaction of other mice to that death. Nature is moving waters of activity. A concerto, with each crescendo and decrescendo a concentric ring of action and reaction, recorded in the track. The track is a universe in itself, reaching beyond its own parameters to encompass the grander universe of all things. Nothing can move in nature without affecting everything else. Waves touching waves, generating currents, creating ripples of all movement, in this interplay of moving water we call life.

Yet awareness and tracking go beyond the physical. Grandfather once said, "Awareness is the doorway to the spirit." A track is not only a window to the past but a doorway to an animal's very soul. The challenge is to step through that doorway.

When we track, we pick up a string. At the far end of the string a being is moving, existing, still connected to the track that we gaze upon. The animal's movement is still contained in that track, along with the smallest of external and internal details. As we follow these tracks, we begin to become the very animal we track. We can feel its hunger, its apprehension, and its movements deep within our own consciousness. We soon find that our body reacts to these movements. Soon our spirit mingles with that of the animal and we lose our isolated human identity. We become the animal, and a deep spiritual bonding and communication begins. We are at once tracking the animal and being tracked by ourselves. Our consciousness becomes so fused with that of the animal that we lose the concept of the track and become the movement itself.

Our awareness expands from the animal we have become to the landscape it reacted to and is played by. We feel the influence of all things that surround us and our awareness expands from our consciousness to the mind of the animal and finally to the very cosmos. We move through the tracks and the tracks move through us. We become, forever, every track we explore and every trail we follow. Each is a mystery in itself, which also unlocks the mysteries of life. To track, then, is not only to know the animal in that point in time, but to touch eternity.

In tracking and awareness, then, there can never be a separation. One without the other is but half a story, an incomplete picture, thus an incomplete understanding. With tracking we unlock the nuances and secrets of each animal we follow, eventually knowing that animal like a brother or a sister. The more we know, the more we see that animal, the more we become. Awareness is evident not only in the number of animals we see, but in our feeling about their interrelationship with all things around them. A relationship to the grand fabric of consciousness we call the spirit-that-moves-through-all-things. It is the track that connects us to that grand consciousness and expands us to limitless horizons.

2. THE EYE OF THE TRACKER

To say that Grandfather observed the world differently from everyone else is a severe understatement. Certainly his perceptions on a spiritual level far surpassed everyone I have ever met or even read about, but equally remarkable was his intense level of awareness and observation on a physical level. Even what the fictitious Sherlock Holmes or the highly technical and scientific FBI crime scene analysts find pale in comparison to what Grandfather would see in a quick glance. Grandfather often stated that awareness is the doorway to the spirit, and I believe he felt that before passing through that doorway one had to be extremely aware on a physical level first. I know that Grandfather demanded of me a high level of physical awareness before he would even venture lessons into the spirit realm. So integral to the spiritual domains was this intense level of physical awareness that Grandfather told us that the best way to identify a spiritual fraud was to determine how aware he or she was on a physical level. Lack of awareness on a physical level was tantamount to no spiritual ability.

As I discussed in the last chapter, to Grandfather, awareness and tracking were one and the same thing. One could not exist without the other. The more one could read the tracks, signs, and the infinite variety of other messages from the landscape, the more aware of the whole one would become. Often, to push our awareness to a higher level, Grandfather would take us deeper into the track and the tracking philosophy. This tracking philosophy aimed to develop the "eye of the tracker," as he called it, which was an intense way of looking at and understanding the land. To have the "eye of the tracker" was to glean immense amounts of information from the land with just a quick glance. To the uninitiated that ability can seem miraculous.

We were introduced to the concepts and philosophy of the "eye of the tracker" through two simple questions: "What happened here?" and "What is this telling me?" Grandfather used these questions to begin our journey into the profound state of awareness that was the hallmark of the "eye of the tracker." Wherever we explored, wherever we went, we were to hold these questions foremost in our minds. It was not limited to the tracks printed on the ground but extended far beyond into the grand world of creation. In fact, the tracks that we found on the ground were just a small part of the answers.

My first encounter with these questions and the "eye of the tracker"

13

did not come in the form of a spoken lesson, but in an example set forth by Grandfather.

We were camped in an area of the Pine Barrens that was new to us. After Rick and I prepared our primitive camp and built our shelters we went exploring, a journey that took the rest of the day and evening. We traveled far, trying to take in everything we could. We followed one track after another, determined not to return until we knew the new area well. Our thirst for adventure, excitement, and exploration was insatiable and this new part of the Pine Barrens was a limitless supply of spiritual water for our thirsting souls. Only the onset of darkness, hunger, and the need to talk to Grandfather about our finds drew us back to camp. Even with all those compelling reasons to return, we turned back reluctantly.

We found Grandfather sitting by the fire working on a buckskin pouch. We noticed that at his side were his bowl and wooden spoon. By the looks of it, he had already eaten. We were upset that we had missed dinner; not only were we starving, but Grandfather's cooking was always exceptionally good. I approached him sheepishly and said that I was sorry for being late for dinner, and just as sheepishly asked him if there was any more. Grandfather looked at Rick and me and, knowing our hunger and disappointment, he giggled to himself. "There is food for you over at the site of the big grandfather pine," he said as he motioned to the distant end of camp, and then went back to working on his bag. Rick and I were relieved that we did not have to forage for dinner and immediately headed off in the direction Grandfather had pointed.

When we got to the edge of camp we suddenly realized that there was no grandfather pine in this area. All of the trees here had been destroyed by fire a long time ago, and the new forest had no trees over twenty feet tall. We did not want to embarrass ourselves, so we searched the far end of camp for the grandfather pine, figuring that we had somehow missed it when we first went exploring. Our search proved futile, for there was no pine of the "grandfather" status anywhere to be found. Still not wanting to give up and return to camp, we searched the entire perimeter and beyond to no avail. We were forced to return to Grandfather empty-handed.

We slipped into camp and sat by the fire, afraid and embarrassed to say a word. Without looking up Grandfather asked us how we had enjoyed our dinner. He knew damn well that we hadn't found the tree or our dinner. Somewhere in all of this, I thought, there had to be a lesson. Rick finally spoke up and admitted that we could not find the grandfather tree. Grandfather only giggled. I became a little frustrated with his game and, spurred by hunger, I told him that there was no grandfather tree. That the area had been destroyed many years ago and only smaller trees surrounded the camp. Without a word, Grandfather stood and began to walk to the far end of camp, motioning us to follow. I worried all the way that somehow we had missed the old pine and we would never live down the failure.

Grandfather led us a short way into the forest then abruptly stopped. Turning to us, he asked, "What are we standing in?"

I answered him quickly and confidently. "A small clearing!"

He then asked, "What is strange about these small trees around the clearing?" We looked for a long time but said nothing. I couldn't understand what he was getting at or what he wanted us to see. Finally, and almost by accident, I noticed that none of the small pine trees around the clearing had branches on the side facing the clearing. Instead, all the branches, except for the uppermost, faced away from the clearing. I told Grandfather about my observation and in the moonlight I could see him smile, apparently satisfied with my answer. He then proceeded to walk back to camp.

I was baffled and asked him about the grandfather pine. He smiled and said, "You already told me where the old tree is, now find your food."

"I did not!" I said, now rather frustrated with this game of his.

"Why do you think there are no lower branches facing the clearing on these smaller pines?" he asked seriously. I thought for a moment then said, "They were blocked from the sun so they did not grow out on that side."

"And what blocked them from the sun?" The answer had now become painfully obvious. "The grandfather pine!" I shouted, and we ran to the center of the clearing. There on the ground was our dinner, just as Grandfather had said it would be, at the site of the old grandfather pine.

Grandfather wandered off to camp and we stood there feasting on our dinner in silence, gazing up into the trees that surrounded the clearing. Upon our return to camp, Grandfather sat us down and said, "The clearing and the small trees are tracks, just like the tracks of animals and man imprinted in the earth. Like all tracks, these little trees are concentric rings, telling of things that are around them now and things that influenced them in the past. Just as the scars on the pines tell you of past fires, now the growth of the trees tells you even more. It tells you of an old pine that long since passed into the spirit world and is now the dust of the earth. All plants, all landscapes, all things then are tracks. We must also look beyond the obvious and ask ourselves, 'What has happened here?' or 'What is this telling me?' " That was the very first time we heard those questions. Questions that would follow us the rest of our lives. It was the beginning of our learning to see with the "eye of the tracker."

From that day on, Rick and I began to see tracking differently. All of creation became a track. Everything on the landscape cried out to us, giving us clues to its mysteries and secrets, hidden to even the few that ventured into the woods. Grandfather continually asked us questions whenever we walked. Questions like, "What is this plant telling you about the soil?" or "Why is this tree growing in this way?" or "Why is there a small hill here?" His questions were designed not only to make us think and to search the landscape on a deeper level, but also to ensure that those questions would remain paramount in our consciousness whether he was with us or not.

When we began to observe the world with that kind of questioning mind, all of nature presented an exciting mystery. And where there is mystery there is always adventure. The countless mysteries and subsequent adventures that we now realized could be found throughout the surrounding landscape made us want to examine all around us. We wanted to integrate the questioning awareness into our everyday activities, even though that day we were confined to the area of the camp. It made no difference to us how well we thought we knew an area, for there were always new things to discover, new depths to explore. Nothing would ever again seem commonplace.

Many months after Grandfather first taught us the lesson of the grandfather pine, thereby introducing questioning awareness to our everyday thinking, he took us into another world of awareness—by focusing our questioning awareness on man.

We were hiking a well-worn hunters' path near the edge of the Pine Barrens when Grandfather suddenly sat down alongside the trail. Without hesitation, especially because we were tired from the trek, we sat down also. Grandfather picked up a crushed cigarette butt and held it up to us. "Did a man or a woman put out this cigarette?" he asked. "Were they right- or left-handed? What emotional state were they in when they put it out? How strong were they?" As the questions continued, our heads reeled with overload and disbelief.

Without waiting for a response he stood and walked to a nearby tree where he pointed to a cut limb. "Was this cut with a knife, machete, saw, axe, or hatchet? How sharp was the cutting implement? Was it a man or a woman who did the cutting? How tall were they? How strong were they? Were they right- or left-handed?" Expecting no response, he pointed to a discarded can on the ground. "Was this dropped or thrown down? Was the person moving when it was dropped or thrown? If thrown, then from where? How strong was the person who drank from this can and how long ago did it end up here?" Again the barrage of questions seemed limitless and overwhelming. He finally pointed to the very trail we walked upon and asked, "Was this trail cut in or worn into the earth? How long has it been a trail and what drew people to create a trail here and not over there? How frequently is it used and what is the season it is most used in?" So many questions and we had no answers, but I don't think Grandfather expected any.

It was obvious what Grandfather was trying to tell us. The actions of people are important too and we should not overlook them with our new-found questioning awareness. We knew we had a lot of work ahead of us, the kind of close observation work that nature presented, only this time with the human animal. Rick and I spent the next several weeks watching people put out cigarette butts, discard cans, throw down garbage, cut trees, brush, limbs, and lawns. People became another major source of study to us and we applied the same vigorous scrutiny to that study as we used with the natural world. Like nature, the world of humankind and its actions was not only a source of fascination but filled with mysteries that had to be solved. It was not as adventurous, though, as the exploration of the natural haunts of creation.

Several months after he initially asked us about the cigarette butt, Grandfather and I were walking the same old hunters' trail when I sat down along the trail. Grandfather sat down also, an inquisitive look on his face. I picked up a discarded cigarette butt. "This was put out by a man who was right-handed and quite strong, as you can see by the finger dents and over-crushed paper ends. The man was probably wrapped deep in thought about other things, for he used more time than was necessary to crush the butt, which is indicative of a thoughtful state of consciousness." I gestured at the trail and added, "This trail has been worn into the ground and not plowed, for there is no berm along the sides. Instead, the trail is deeper than the surrounding landscape. It was originally a well-used deer trail, judging by how it winds through and interacts with the landscape. A trail created solely by man is straighter."

I then pointed to the cut limb that Grandfather had pointed out months earlier. "Right-handed teenage boy, using a dull saw. He has little experience with cutting of any sort and the limb was almost out of his reach, judging from the sloppiness and changing angles of the cut. These angles depict someone standing on tiptoes and frequently losing his balance. He is also quite weak for a teenager and probably doesn't engage in much physical activity. Though, I still cannot figure out why he cut the limb in the first place."

Grandfather smiled a grand smile of approval and pride at what I had done. "He was using it as a way to mark the trail so he would not get lost," he explained. "As you can see far up ahead, more limbs have been cut, and trees blazed to help him find his way back out." We both laughed long and hard with joy at my success.

Yet my lessons with the human animal and nature did not end there. Questioning awareness led to experimentation and acute observation. Rick and I would spend hours throwing cans to various heights, from various angles, and at various speeds. We then went over and saw what marks they left. We watched people secretly, not only in the woods but going about their daily lives in the confines of society. We watched the games they played, what they observed and what they didn't. We observed what they reacted to and what they missed or overlooked. We watched how they tied their shoes, combed their hair, what clothing they wore in what weather, and the wear marks on clothing caused by various professions. We watched their tracks and learned how different professions and interests create different tracks, different moods, and different states of awareness. Our observation of humans, however, intense though it was, could never come close to the time and energy we put into the study of nature.

Month after month, year in and year out, Grandfather added new realms and levels of awareness to our questioning consciousness. We repeated learning exercises dozens, even hundreds of times, until we could glean volumes of information at a mere glance. We pushed deeper and deeper into the levels of awareness and reveled in the staggering information that each square inch of nature would provide. A pebble slightly moved in its bed, a missing drop of rain at the end of a twig, a crushed fragment of grit, and the flatness of dust held countless secrets and revealed to us immense amounts of information.

Thus, the "eye of the tracker" became our way, forever embedded into our consciousness. Today I walk from my front door to the lecture area of my school. A distance of no more than fifty yards, yet to me it is an infinite journey. Even rushed by intense lecture schedules I can see where rabbits fed in my front yard, where a raccoon foraged near the bird feeder, where a weasel killed a mouse at the corner of an old stone wall, where a fox meandered down my driveway, where two deer walked through the students' sleeping area, where a barn owl came to rest momentarily on an old fencepost, and where an old skunk emerged from under the barn. This is not to mention the innumerable mice, birds, and insects and countless other mysteries observed and solved. Yet this observation is done before I get to the lecture hall without hesitation or breaking my stride. All is gathered at a glance through the "eye of the tracker."

This is the same level of understanding and awareness that all trackers must achieve in order to become "master" trackers. They must develop that questioning awareness, following mystery after mystery until all secrets are revealed. The mind must be trained to penetrate the obvious and reach deep into the intricate levels of awareness. There is not a moment in the day, whether in nature or the city, that the questions "What happened here?" and "What is this telling me?" are not foremost on my mind. Master trackers do not look at life, nature, or anything, for that matter, superficially. Everywhere there are mysteries to be solved and the land calls out with concentric rings telegraphing the present and the past. Master trackers are never satisfied with the way that even the most accomplished naturalist views the world. We must penetrate beyond even intense awareness and see the world as Grandfather saw it. Only then can we hope to fuse our consciousness with that of the natural world and beyond, to that of the spirit.

3. THE MASTER TRACKER

To Grandfather's mind there were just two types of trackers, those he called "typical" or "common" trackers and those he called "master" trackers. He was very quick to point out the difference in these two approaches to tracking and made it very clear to us that he intended to teach us to be master trackers. Common trackers, he told us, followed a string of lifeless depressions in the ground to get to an animal. They could tell very little about a track other than the relative age of the imprint and the approximate size of the animal. They frequently lost the trail, because they were never taught to see tracks in anything other than soft ground. They were also very slow because they had no concept of the broader, more demanding form of tracking.

Master trackers, on the other hand, were creatures of intense detail. A master tracker could read the tracks of all animals on any surface, even solid rock. To the master tracker, the tracks were not just a string of lifeless depressions strewn across the ground, but a window to an animal's very soul. Each track contains within its boundaries a miniature topographic map, a map that reveals its maker's innermost secrets. Absorbed in such detail and obsessed with intense training, the master tracker could track even the smallest insect across solid rock surfaces, deep forest litter, and even grasslands. It was inconceivable that a master tracker would ever lose a trail, unless that trail were completely erased by weathering or destroyed by other animals walking over it.

The road to becoming a master tracker was filled with wonder, but it was also endlessly difficult and tedious work. So intense was our training that within the first six months we were tracking mice across gravel beds, and before the end of the first year we were tracking ants across stone. Little did we realize at the time that this type of tracking was only the beginning of what we were yet to learn, of the depths we would eventually see. Grandfather told us that in his tribe children younger than five could follow the tracks of mice across solid rock. By the age of six they could follow ants across the same rock. Yet this only qualified them to be considered common trackers.

I vividly remember my first lesson into the depths of what a master tracker observes in a track. This level of observation is incomprehensible to even the most experienced trackers today, but commonplace to the children of Grandfather's tribe. At the time, Rick and I were attempting to track ants ants across a dry gravel bed. We could see the ants' tracks on the outer perimeter of that gravel bed easily because a fine coating of dusty soil framed the tracks. This silty dust border was the best of tracking soils, but as soon as the ant tracks hit the gravel, we lost them immediately. We tried and tried again to follow numerous ant trails into the gravel, but could not find even one single print. For hours we kept up this fruitless struggle to find the next track. The frustration level became unbearable.

We were so intent on our tracking and wrapped up in trying to find the next track that we failed to notice Grandfather watching us. Suddenly his voice shattered our concentration and jolted us back to the grander world outside the track. He said, "Do not get so absorbed in the track that you lose your place in the oneness. By limiting your vision to the track, you also limit your senses, and your awareness does not reach beyond that track. You are thus imprisoned by the track and limited only to the trail. Nothing else exists for you outside of your track and you lose consciousness of the spirit-that-moves-through-all-things. You then only understand nature in fragments and never fully comprehend the larger realms of the universe. By fragmentation and absorption in a single track, you diminish your tracking ability. All tracks should be viewed as concentric rings, influenced and influencing the worlds beyond. A track is the beginning and the ending of all concentric rings. Vary then your vision from the tracks and stay conscious of the worlds beyond."

Grandfather was right. So many times before we had made that same mistake, and the track had become a vacuum, sucking in and imprisoning our consciousness. By not looking from the track to the larger world beyond, we missed what was going on and fragmented the whole; thus, we hindered our tracking abilities. Yet, it was very hard for me not to become absorbed in the track, to remain aware of everything else. After all, tracking was my obsession. My passion for the mystery of the track would rarely let my awareness go beyond the boundaries of the track. I had made that mistake over and over without fail. Even the embarrassment of having Grandfather walk right up on me was not enough to keep me from my consuming track obsession. I just could not let go and expand, the way Grandfather wanted me to.

Without saying another word about my absorption, Grandfather said, "Look at the gravel rocks and tell me what you see." I looked close and hard at the stones but did not have a clue as to what Grandfather wanted me to see. I tried to venture a guess about the stones being pushed down in their beds. But since we were tracking ants I knew that just could not be. Exasperated, I asked Grandfather what he wanted me to see. He simply said, "Look what is on the gravel rocks, not at the gravel rocks." I searched again, determined not to fail, but again I could not understand what he wanted. Just as I was about to give up I suddenly understood what he was saying. "Dust and grit particles are covering the rocks!" I was amazed at my own statement because I never thought about it before it was out of my mouth.

Grandfather chuckled at my astonished expression. "What is it about small areas of the dust that is different from the whole?" Looking closely at what first appeared to be an even coating of dust, I soon found that small areas were dented into the dust, thus flattening it completely. The areas were only the size that the point of a pin would make, but they were clear, especially when the rock was held between myself and the sun.

I looked at Grandfather and said, "Why, the dust is flattened in little places all along the top of the rock!"

"Yes, Grandson," Grandfather said, "Those are the tracks of the ants you have been trying to follow." I was amazed beyond words. I had tracked an ant across a gravel rock and hadn't realized that I was doing it. I was so interested in the flattened dust that I didn't realized that it had been flattened by ant feet.

Grandfather then said, "If you are looking at the flatness of dust, you are looking many times too large. To a master tracker, flattened dust is a major track indicator. You must learn now to look smaller, to a level that is out of your grasp right now." Grandfather walked away and I lay on the ground in silence. The near microscopic level of dust was the smallest I had ever dreamed of looking. I could not imagine worlds beyond that tiny level. Without hesitation or asking Grandfather for more, I tracked ants across the gravel rocks for the rest of the day. With each successful trail completed, the tracks grew clearer, until I reached the point where I came to view the dust flatness as a major track. As the setting sun put an end to my ant tracking for the day I now could imagine a world smaller than the dust depressions, but I had no idea as to how to get there.

As Grandfather had said, the flattened dust was indeed a major track indicator, a huge sign for a master tracker. Rick and I learned in the following months to look for slight discolorations in rocks, vegetation, or forest litter that would indicate pressure from an animal foot, thus a track. We kept pushing ourselves to attain infinitely smaller levels of track observation. However, Grandfather would never permit us to use a magnifying glass; he said it would become a self-limiting crutch. We had to train our eyes to know not only what to look at, but how to see. We varied the light sources, changed our angles, looked high and low, and used all manner of other actions to enhance even the smallest track. We had become creatures that thrived on intense detail.

This attention to minute detail was both a blessing and a curse. I became more and more absorbed in the track to the exclusion of everything else. Tracks became a prison for my awareness and I missed so much else. Little did I realize that by being absorbed in the track, I was missing the greater picture of what tracking was all about. No matter how many times Grandfather warned me, I could not free myself of certain tracks. When there was an intense mystery to be solved or a deeper level to look, I disappeared into the track. Many times I would be tracking Grandfather and pass right by him without noticing as he stood by watching me. Once when I was tracking a deer I took a break to stretch and, looking behind me, saw that the deer had crossed the trail a few feet away from me. No amount of warning or humiliation could free me totally from my passion for certain tracks. It wasn't until long after Grandfather had gone on his final walk to the spirit world that I finally learned this lesson.

Another time, I was involved in tracking a murder suspect who was believed to have killed his brother, wife, and mother; he had disappeared off into the woods after his car was pulled over by the State Police. For the better part of a week, the police searched for him to no avail. The suspect had been an avid hunter, survivalist, and mercenary. He successfully eluded the police and pressed deeper into the woods. There was no doubt in anyone's mind that he could easily survive in the wilderness for a long period of time, given his training. Rumors about this man's talents abounded. Rumors even the police began to believe. By the time I was called into the case, paranoia was running deep among the searchers. Fear of the suspect's ability to turn the tables on the trackers was causing the investigation to fall apart. They were desperate to try something new so they called on me.

Though I had successfully tracked down several hundred lost or fugitive people by this time in my life and had a considerable reputation among law enforcement agencies, my arrival at the scene was met with the usual skepticism. Many of the officers could not see how I was going to do any good, especially since the suspect had evaded even their best bloodhounds. As is typical of the untutored, they just didn't understand tracking. Within an hour of being dropped off in the backwoods by a helicopter, I had located the suspect's trail. As I followed him I quickly lost my backup, which is also typical on a tracking case. Even people with considerable training have a hard time keeping up with a good tracker.

By the third hour of tracking I had closed to within a half hour of the suspect. It had become clear to me that this guy was by far not the competent woodsman that he was rumored to be. This is usually the case with modern survivalist types. Without his guns and modern technical equipment, he was totally out of place. The only thing that he had on him of any consequence was the .38 revolver he was said to have used to kill his victims. Judging from the tracks, he was hopelessly lost, frightened, disoriented, hungry, thirsty, and very tired. This was definitely to my advantage, for without my backup it would be difficult for me to apprehend him, especially since I never carry a gun when I track. This suspect was also out of his mind with paranoia, which added to the intensity of the tracking situation.

Moving very cautiously, now I began to close the gap. I could not afford any mistakes, nor could I let him know that he was being followed. As far as he was concerned he'd escaped the police, and now his greatest enemy was the wilderness. The longer I tracked him, however, the more complacent I became. His tracks were showing his ineptness in the wilderness in a big way. He was a fish out of water and he knew it. Panic was beginning to set in to his mind, causing him to make foolish mistakes. His tracks showed him jolting this way and that, reacting to the various noises of the forest. To him, his only link to sanity was his gun. Without that gun he would certainly perish. It became his lifeline, and now he held it in front of him as he walked, ready to shoot anything that moved.

Suddenly his tracks began to do strange things. I could not figure out what was going on in his mind. His blundering panic blurred any rational explanation of what was troubling him. In my complacency over this suspect's ability, and lured by the troubling tracks, I made a near fatal mistake. I became absorbed by his trail. I wanted to figure out what was going on in his mind. Now, within only five minutes of his position, I lost all sense of time and place. I got down on my hands and knees to study the tracks in an attempt to unlock the mystery. It was not long before the track became a prison to my awareness. I searched every facet of the track, looking for clues, for thought imprints. Searching my mind for similar past tracks that might have been like this one in some way.

Then, as my eyes looked into the toe section of the bootprint, the intent became clear. I had seen this kind of movement and pattern in a track before, though at first I had to search my memory for detail. Finally I remembered. It was a "realization" print. The suspect at this point knew he was being followed. With this shocking enlightenment I clearly heard Grandfather's voice say, "Vary your vision!" It was at that precise moment, as my awareness expanded and complacency vanished, that I felt someone standing behind me. The rest happened so quickly that still in recollection it is all a blur. With a nerve-shattering explosion from the gun, I was shot in the back.

If I had been still bent over the track at the time the gun was fired, I would have been shot in the back of the head, which was the intent. If I had come to a full standing position at that moment, I would have been crippled from the waist down. But with the spirit of Grandfather's voice and the sudden "Inner Vision" both telling me that someone was behind me, I stood and started to turn. The bullet caught me just above the belt line and traveled under my skin like a splinter before exiting neatly. Except for a stinging, burning sensation I was unhurt. Surprised by my abrupt movement up from the track, the suspect could not get off a second shot. Instead I was on him immediately in the most vicious display of Apache "wolverine fighting" that I can remember.

To this day I carry with me that neat little .38 scar in my back. It has become a constant reminder that the secrets held within the borders of a track are only a small part of the story. With each track we must keep our awareness moving from the track to the universe and back again. The day I stopped becoming so absorbed in a track was the day that my tracking ability grew exponentially. Master trackers are creatures of intense detail but even the most minute detail must lead to the whole of creation. The consciousness of a master tracker, then, must lead from a grain of silt pressed within a track to the very horizon and beyond.

4. THE SCIENCE AND ART OF TRACKING

Many students come to my school feeling that tracking, at least the kind of tracking Grandfather taught, is out of reach. They wrongly assume that it takes some superhuman eyesight and senses keener than those of mortal man to reach the deeper levels of tracking they read about in my books. This is just not true. When I say that tracking is a science and art, I don't mean to imply that it is the kind of art in which someone has to be born gifted or talented to obtain excellence. With the proper training and dedication one need not be gifted in arts such as painting, music, poetry, and sculpting to enjoy them. Of course being born with a talent surely helps. But in tracking, I believe that everyone has the innate talent. After all, one of my best trackers is legally blind and must track solely with his hands.

The art of tracking grows from a passion for learning that borders on obsession. A love of tracking and the passion for solving mysteries are enough for anyone to reach the deeper levels of tracking. Yet it is not so important that you feel that passion immediately. This is something that develops from deep within, born from a basic knowledge of tracking at first. Thus, one's passion and love for tracking will build as one's level of understanding and skill grows. Anyway, I don't really know what special talent a person can be born with to make him or her a great tracker. Tracking, after all, is embedded in our genes, a part of our heritage. Generations of our ancestors used it in their hunting and gathering lifestyle. Man has held a club in his hand longer then he has held a pen.

Somewhere, deep inside everyone, are the seeds of passion for tracking. It is my job to impart the knowledge that will awaken that passion. Learning tracking techniques is the same as learning any fine art. The techniques I share stir the artist within, opening up the right brain, that part of ourselves that deals not with linear thought, words, or mathematics, but rather with patterns, colors, textures, and other artistic endeavors. One finds that the techniques and theories that help a person paint better, write fine music, or sculpt are the same techniques that help a person see tracks and track patterns better. This is why I refer to tracking as an art.

Yet I could also call tracking a philosophy and a deep form of spiritual communication. First we enter the world of tracking as a science, in which we learn all the cold, hard facts about the track. These basic techniques must be understood before any further building can be done. Then, and only then, can tracking develop into an art, where one begins to see the

27

beauty of the tracks. This mastery of the artistic form then leads to the more spiritual aspects of tracking. Spiritual tracking is what Grandfather deemed the most important. It is here in the spiritual consciousness where the animal comes alive in its tracks. It is here that we fuse our mind with the animal and feel the animal moving within us. Finally we become that animal, moved by its spirit.

But the fact remains that we must first enter the world of tracking through its science. As I stated before, the more one knows about the mechanics and techniques of tracking, the more one is impassioned. It is this impassioned self that transcends the physical mechanics of tracking, and becomes the art and the spirit. Tracking then moves from outside the self, where we view the land from a perspective of isolation and separation, to a point were we track from within. There is not, nor can there be, any separation. It becomes important that the new tracker never lose sight of the artistic and spiritual goals as he or she is working on the mechanics of tracking. Without a strong foundation in the tracking science principles, the spirit of tracking can never be achieved.

Once the science is understood and internalized, the subsequent artistic and spiritual approaches need not be taught. The transition from science, to art, then to spirit is a natural progression. This transition, this meta-morphosis, is something that just happens and can never be taught. The science of tracking is like a seed. That seed is sustained by the life-giving forces of the art, which then gives birth to the growth of spirit. Without the seed there can be nothing. Without the soil and sustaining forces there can be nothing. Each depends on the other to bring about this higher growth of consciousness.

While the art and spirit of tracking are effortless, the science of tracking requires considerable "dirt time," as I call it. Dirt time is the time spent looking at the ground, at tracks, using the mechanics of tracking. This dirt time requires no special inborn gift. Instead, it takes a dogged determina-tion. That determination is the child of passion. As passion grows, so does the determination. There is no bypassing dirt time; it is necessary for achiev-ing excellence. Yet, thanks to the accumulation of knowledge passed down to us from Grandfather, our dirt time is not only more productive and exciting, but cut to a bare minimum of time.

Grandfather never made it easy for Rick or me. After all, he had only two students and over ten years to teach us. Much of his teaching was designed to make us think, to learn from our mistakes, and to find answers for ourselves. He did not try to simplify or expedite anything for us, but expected us right from the start to find the passion in ourselves. He was a Coyote teacher, which is another way of saying we learned through dirt time, and lots of it. Most times he would give us just a little hint about a technique and allow us to go figure it out for ourselves. When we finally reached an unbearable level of frustration and failure, he would finish the lesson and give us the rest of the answer. He was always there for us, guiding, nurturing, and teaching. Nevertheless, it was still hard work and long hours. He expected nothing less. If we were ever to show disinterest, complacency, or lack of passion, he would just not teach us again. We had to want it badly and show him our desire to learn through our dogged determination.

Within the confines of this book, I do not have the luxury to be a Coyote teacher. Everything must be spelled out precisely and simplified. Thus, many of the lessons that we had to learn the hard way, through dirt time, must be bypassed and the final answers given immediately. I can't be there to see if you are impassioned and determined to reach tracking excellence. You have to find it within yourself through the knowledge set forth in this book. In the final analysis you must put in the dirt time and, though it will not take as much time as it did for me, dirt time is still a reality. Only you can develop that determination and drive, that passion, and that commitment to excellence. I can only give you the tools you need to learn. The rest is up to you.

One of the most powerful lessons Grandfather ever taught me concerning determination and dirt time came only a few weeks after I met Grandfather, and the impact of that lesson lasted a lifetime. Grandfather, Rick, and I had traveled to an entirely new area to camp, an area the likes of which we had never seen before. Here the forest met huge estuaries— the place was overflowing with wildlife and plant life in great diversity. It beckoned us to explore and promised an endless source of adventure. Soon after our arrival I spotted a mink track and went to investigate. I knew that it was a mink track but I did not know how old it was. I asked Grandfather to come look at the track and I asked him how long ago the mink had made it.

Grandfather looked up from the track and spotted a deer walking along the tree line in the distance. He motioned to me to follow, obviously not answering my question about the mink, or possibly, I thought, forgetting about it completely. We arrived at the fresh deer tracks and Grandfather led me to one in particular. He instructed me to lie down beside the track. I did, and I found that it was in the same type of soil as was the mink track.

Grandfather then said, "This track will teach you the age of the mink tracks." He then walked back to camp, leaving me confused as to how this track was going to teach me about the age of the mink track.

I lay on my belly for the better part of two hours, paying more attention to what was going on in the camp than to the deer track. I desperately wanted to go out and spend the day exploring the new area around camp and was beginning to feel imprisoned by the track. I grew restless and angry. I began to feel that this was some sort of punishment, Grandfather's way of getting rid of me and my questions for a while as he went out and had fun exploring and having adventures with Rick. A cloud of jealousy began to overtake me, for Rick was still free to do what he wanted and I was feeling very left out. I glanced back at the deer track and could not see what Grandfather wanted me to see. It looked as fresh as ever. Two hours was long enough for this, I thought, and headed back to camp.

I found Grandfather sitting near camp by the same mink track I had asked him about. As I approached I could sense that Grandfather was a little disappointed with me. Before I could say a word to him, he pointed down to the mink track and asked, "How old is this track?" Of course I had no idea and, after squirming a bit, I whispered sullenly, "I don't know." Grandfather's stare seemed to pierce my very soul and I could feel his displeasure. He finally said, "Apparently, Grandson, the age of this mink track is not important to you. I can't teach you any more until you learn the age of this track and tracks like it. You seem to want things handed to you without working for them. You want things easy. It is obvious that you do not love tracking enough."

Grandfather solemnly stood, gathered his things, and headed toward the trail that led back to his own camp, which was many miles away. Just before he disappeared from sight, he called out to me, "When you love tracking enough and are willing to dedicate the time, then and only then will I teach you. I will teach no more until you prove you want to learn, no matter what the hardship." His words cut deep and tears welled up in my eyes as I watched him disappear down the distant trail. Rick was nowhere to be found and I felt so alone and hurt. I did know, though, that my hurt was of my own doing, it was my own fault. I knew this very well. Grandfather had never taught anything in the past that we did not desperately want to learn, but we had to reach that point first. I had shown no desperation—barely an interest—and I could not blame Grandfather.

I went back to the deer track and lay for the rest of the day watching the weather work its magic. As the day shifted to night I built a small fire close by so that I could watch the track degrade through the evening. Magically, I became absorbed by this grain-by-grain deterioration of the track. The track became a miniature mandalla that absorbed my consciousness. Time flew by and my enthusiasm grew exponentially. I watched that track for hours into the night. Intermittently I built up the fire and hurried back to the track. I was so interested in what I was doing that I forgot to eat or even drink. I paid no attention to the chill of the night, the dew that settled on my back and legs, or the cold that seeped into my body. Not even Rick's enthusiastic urging that we go for a night hike could tear me away from the track.

I awoke to a brilliant dawn, frozen to the core, wet from dew, and bewildered about where I was. I looked back at the track, which had now gone through significant changes—changes that came close to the level of deterioration I'd seen in the mink track. I was riveted again to the track, ignoring both hunger and the cold that wracked my body. Slowly, the deer track began to wilt as dew dried from its walls and seemed to melt into the floor. The sun was well up in the sky when the track finally reached the same level of degradation and patina as the mink's had been when I found it the day before. I jumped to my feet in triumph, unable to contain my enthusiasm and yelling out that the mink track was made exactly a day before the deer track, within the same hour. I called out to everything and no one.

Suddenly I heard Grandfather's voice behind me saying, "Now you are ready to learn!" I turned with a jolt, shocked by the sudden appearance of Grandfather. "You are only off by a little, Grandson," he continued. "You forget that your fire accelerated the drying process because it was a little close to the track. But now you know how old the mink track is, wisdom that can't be taught by anyone, except by the track itself. As with so many other tracking lessons, no one can really teach you the aging process of tracks. All it takes to learn then is a love of tracking and a determination to find out for yourself, no matter how much time it takes." He paused for a long moment then said, "Let's go now and explore."

I was both elated and relieved by what Grandfather had said. Our day of exploration was an endless string of exciting adventures, yet it paled in comparison to what the track had taught me. An understanding of the aging process had developed and I began to see all the tracks I encountered that day in a new light. I could determine the age of many of those tracks to within a few hours—much to the annoyance of Rick, who could not. Yet, even with that success, I knew that I had a long, hard road ahead of me. I had much to learn about aging tracks, but I learned all I needed to know about what Grandfather expected of me. He expected a passion that bordered on obsession for tracking, an intense interest that even transcended a love of tracking.

There is no replacement for dirt time. Certainly, when you are finished with this book, with hardly any dirt time at all, you will be a great tracker. A deeper understanding of the track and a new way of looking at tracks will be yours. But if you are to become an awesome tracker, then you have to put in the dirt time. All I can do is give you the tools and skills necessary to make your dirt time more productive. I cannot give you the passion, the love, or the obsession it takes to become an awesome tracker. Only you can do that. Yet I am confident that the more you learn about tracking and the more you see through the "eye of the tracker," the more you will seek the dirt time. Tracking is a science, an art and a spiritual journey, a journey that you can only take when you commit yourself to the track.

5. INTRODUCTION TO PRESSURE RELEASES

Before we enter into a physical definition and the mechanics of pressure releases, let's first consider the spiritual concept of tracking. As I stated earlier, tracking is not merely the act of following lifeless depressions across the ground. Nor is it simply a means to follow or find game. To the Apache Scouts, this basic tracking concept was far too limited. It was not even the beginning. Tracking was their window to the wilderness and they trusted this skill with their very lives. Their skill as trackers was developed to such a high degree that it far surpassed that of the best trackers found throughout the world. To the Scout, tracking was far more than the physical act of following tracks. It was not only a science and art, but a philosophy unto itself.

I remember once hearing Grandfather say that the best trackers in the world were the Scouts. In fact, in his mind, no other culture of trackers came close. Since I had never been out of the Pine Barrens of New Jersey, and had nothing to compare this statement to, I considered this to be a bold boast on his part. It wasn't until my reputation as a tracker grew, and I began to track lost people and criminals throughout the world, that I realized that Grandfather had been right. In my nearly six hundred tracking cases, having worked with people reputed to be the best trackers in the world, I soon realized that these trackers had no concept of the intense detail and nuances that Grandfather demanded we see in each track. In fact, most of the best trackers I have met could hardly compare to my most basic Standard class graduate's ability.

Even in most rudimentary application of their tracking techniques, the Scouts transcended everyone else's ability. The Apaches were a people of constant migration, which took them to all manner of landscapes, weather conditions, soils, and unique topography. They would move from desert to mesas, to mountains, to forests, to alpine zones, to rocky soils, and even into the plains. They learned to master the tracking of all the landscapes they encountered, even when that landscape was solid rock. Their ability to track in any environment and weather condition pushed them far beyond the normal limitations of tracking and into a separate reality. Equally so, their awareness had also to be pushed to such a height that it surpassed everyone else's. After all, tracking and awareness were considered by Grandfather to be one and the same.

Thus, the basic tracking methods of the Scouts were not confined to one single area or topography, as it was with so many other tribes throughout the world. Their foundation became very broad and all-encompassing. To the Scouts, the safety and survival of their people was closely linked to their tracking and awareness ability. In fact, it was the single most important factor in the Scout's physical life. Yes, they had to learn tracking for practice purposes and out of necessity, but soon the tracking concepts began a metamorphosis that transcended the mere physical applications. Tracking became, for many, a deeply religious and philosophical experience. These philosophic overtones became evident to me right from the beginning. Grandfather would so often relate a tracking technique to an ancient Apache parable or a spiritual teaching. In fact, most of the training of the ancient Scouts revolved around the sacredness of the track and its deep religious overtones. To the Scout, tracks were the first communication received from the Earth. The track became the very voice of the Earth.

I remember Grandfather saying, "Before you can hear the voices of Earth Mother and her animals, you first must listen to the voice of the tracks. It is in the tracks that we first learn to communicate with the animals, not only in a broad sense, but even in intimate detail. To ignore the track is to ignore the first faint voice of creation, and thus we can never hear or fully understand the grander messages of wilderness. So then, we first must learn the simple language of the tracks, which teaches us to hear the voice of the animal, and soon, through the voice of the animal, we begin to hear the voice of the Earth." As a child I began to understand this basic communication almost from the beginning. Through the language of the track, I began to understand the animal, its habits, its movements played out on the landscape, its fears, and eventually its thoughts. It was not long before I knew the animal I tracked like a brother, and not long after our minds fused so that I could feel the animal moving inside of me. I became the animal I tracked, and we were one.

Looking objectively at how closely tied tracking is to both necessity and deep spiritual conviction, one can clearly begin to see the next logical step, the ultimate evolution in tracking, the pressure releases. If a track is the Scout's cathedral, then the pressure releases are the voice of the Creator. That is why I so often say that tracking is not only an art form and a science, but also a philosophy. I learned, even from my earliest lessons, an intense devotion, a sacredness, and a reverence for the tracks. Yes, the Scouts would hold the wisdom of tracking in the same sacred and lofty position that many other tribes would hold the Sacred Pipe, the Sun Dance, or even the Vision Quest.

Over the years I have come to realize the importance of all physical skills in the philosophy of living as one with the Earth. It was not just the skills of tracking and awareness that are important, but also the skills of survival. In the times before the reservations, according to Grandfather, the Native Americans held all practice of the physical skills in the same esteem that they held the highest spiritual ceremonies and sacred objects. As the sacred, religious skills were for the survival of the spirit, the physical skills were for the survival of the flesh. One could not exist without the other, for both were considered to be sacred gifts from the Creator. These gifts had to be respected, cherished, protected, and honored. Thus, even the most common fire-making skill, the making of arrowheads, bows, shelters, and all the rest were honored with the same intense need and sacred respect as the more classically spiritual and religious skills.

Grandfather was appalled whenever he encountered a ceremony where the necessary physical skills had been ignored. To practice just the spiritual skill and leave out the physical skill that should accompany it was to have an incomplete ceremony. At best, this type of neglect would never allow the full spiritual potential of the ceremony to evolve. Grandfather once said, "To light a sacred fire with anything other than the hand-drill or bow-drill is to shun the sacred physical skill given to us by the Creator. Thus, the ceremony will lack the duality, where the skills of the flesh and the skills of the spirit are fused into a sacred oneness. No one should make the choice to embrace one and turn away from the other. Both are gifts of life from the Creator. To set aside one and cling to the other is incomplete and a rejection of the Creator's precious gift. To set aside one is a sacrilege."

Considering the way Grandfather felt about all physical skills, it is easy to see why tracking was held up to such an intense spiritual light. It was one of the most important skills to the Scouts. Not only was it a means of finding game and keeping them from danger, but it was a direct link, a powerful communication with the Earth, and eventually to the spirit. It is with this in mind that we must now go on to a more physical and mechanical approach to tracking. The tracking that the Scouts understood. The power of the pressure releases. Yet, even as we learn the more scientific, mechanical, and physical laws governing the pressure releases, the spiritual applications should never be abandoned. It is through this cold physical approach that we first hear the faint calling of the Earth's voice.

The term *pressure release* is mine alone. Grandfather referred to them as "the voice, or spirit, of the track." My term derives more from Grandfather's full description of the process than from any word or phrase. Grandfather said, "The spirit of the track is formed when the foot pressures the ground, bending and shaping the earth to the rhythm of the body's movements and thoughts. The ground reacts like water, swirling, flowing, building, and ebbing, creating ridges, valleys, pocks, domes, spires, and all manner of other features. Each feature is a reaction to the body and mind of its maker. Yet its fluid movements are not fully born until the pressure is released and the track settles into its full reality. It is then, and only then, that the track is fully born.

"Many will believe that it is the maker of the track who decides the spirit of the track. It is not up to the maker of the track to decide or influence anything. Instead, it is the way the Earth feels about the maker's walk that determines the track's ultimate voice. All things that leave tracks in the flesh of Earth Mother speak the same language when it comes to the spirit of the track. All earth moves the same way, reacts the same way, no matter if man, bear, mouse, or ant makes the track. Movement and pressure create the same effects on the earth, and it is the Earth who makes them reality. It is the Earth who gives the tracks life, spirit, and voice. And it is the release of the pressure that brings it into reality." This was the way Grandfather explained the process to me. This was the genesis of my calling them "pressure releases," but in my heart they are still the "spirit of the track."

In essence, Grandfather was saying that pressure releases are the way the Earth reacts to the maker of a track. In saying that all earth moves the same way, he meant that it does not matter what is making the track, or how the track is being made, or even the physical size of the maker. The earth still reacts in a certain way. The pressure releases left in the tracks of a galloping bear would be the same as the pressure releases left in the tracks of a galloping mouse. Of course, even though the pressure releases would look the same in both, the size of the pressure releases would differ greatly. In proportion to the track, however, these pressure releases would be the same. But now let's back up and lay a more basic foundation for the study of pressure releases.

The feet of any animal, including a human's, are like pedestals. Not only is the foot used for support of the entire body but it is also used in conjunction with the entire body and mind to keep the animal upright and to facilitate all motion. Movement is not as easy and fluid as one might think. Instead it is a series of checks and balances. In order to keep any body upright and moving, especially given the laws of gravity, landscape and wind resistance, fatigue factors, and the many other influences both inside and outside the body, there must be reaction to every action. All actions—and reactions—have to be compensated for through the body and ultimately telegraphed to the feet in order to keep the mechanism of movement in balance. Thus, the feet record not only the action, but also the reaction.

To understand this concept of checks and balances, let's look at an example. If you started in a standing upright position and then bent slowly at the waist to look down at the ground, you would feel your feet flex forward and the balls of your feet pressurize the ground in compensation. If you did not flex your feet and transfer pressure in this way you would quickly lose your balance and fall forward. If you were to pick up a heavy weight, your body would respond by leaning away from the weight and your feet would roll in compensation with your body. Again, if you failed to lean away from the weight you would quickly lose your balance and fall. So too, every action, large or small, has to be compensated for, otherwise the body moves inefficiently and loses balance.

You may be asking yourself, at this point, about my definition of a "small" movement. Well, try this little experiment: Stand barefooted on a cool, bare floor and close your eyes, paying rapt attention to your feet through this entire exercise. Bare feet on a cool floor helps you to pay attention to the slightest movements in the feet. Keep in mind nonetheless that these movements will also show right through the heaviest of shoes or boots. Now, move your right or left hand from your side and touch your nose with your fingertip. You will feel your body and feet respond dramatically to the weight change your lifted arm created. Now move your hand to the top of your head and again you will feel the movement and changes in the feet. Now move the hand to the ear, then finally back to the side. If you have been paying attention you will have easily felt your feet move, pressurize, and compensate for each movement of the arm.

Now let's go a little further, still barefoot and on the cool floor. Again paying rapt attention to your feet, slowly turn your head to the right and then all the way to the left. Here you will also feel the rolling motion of your feet compensating for the movement of your head and body. Going even further into this little experiment, take a moderately deep breath and feel the feet move to compensate for the expansion of the chest and other reactions of the body to that breath. Finally, standing very still, swallow normally. You will be astounded when you feel the dramatic reaction your feet have to this simple act of swallowing. You must remember, however, that this is nothing new to your feet or body. It is just you recognizing the effects for the first time. These effects of your body's actions and reactions have always been there; they have always registered in your tracks. Now that your attention has been drawn to the compensating actions and reactions of your feet, you realize how dramatic and startling those movements are. In essence, what you are feeling when your feet shift to compensate for other movement is the birth of the pressure releases that are found in the track.

Grandfather took this exercise of self-discovery one step further. To show me how sensitive the feet were to even the slightest movement, he had me stand on a log that was suspended across our camp swimming area. Here on this small log, balance was paramount. Any slight movement of my body was magnified. Just the simple act of sticking my tongue out caused a fluctuation in balance that caused my feet to shift dramatically. The sensitivity I felt when standing on that log far surpassed anything I felt on solid ground. I was amazed at how even a gentle whispering breeze could affect the entire balance mechanism of the body and telegraph it to the feet. The same forces that were so powerful on the log were working on solid ground also. Through the log I gained a full understanding of how sensitive these tiny compensating movements could be.

How far does this movement to track sensitivity go? Well beyond the scope of this book. I have an entire series of week-long classes dedicated to this subject alone. But be assured, with the basic pressure release information in this book, you will have the tools to take tracking as far as you want. Not only are the slightest movements of animals and humans registered in the tracks through the pressure releases, but so are thoughts. If an animal even thinks of turning right, for instance, it will register in the track. So too, do emotions, like anger, fear, apprehension, and joy, register in the track. The body reacts to thoughts and emotions in clearly defined pressure release maps. For instance, when you are happy you tend to hold your head up, and conversely, when you are sad you tend to bow the head and slump the shoulders. So it is with all emotion. There is a body reaction that is clearly seen in the track.

The internal condition of the animal or human also shows up in the pressure releases. Through pressure releases we can tell if an animal's belly is full or empty, or partially filled. We can see indicators of thirst or injury. We can also see diseases, for the body also reacts to disease through compensating movements. These pressure release systems are so intricate and defining that you will know more about the animal than you ever dreamed possible. It is like looking into the animal's very soul. Each track tells us everything about that animal: its actions, reactions, its condition, whether it is full or hungry, thirsty or tired, healthy or sick, even what it is thinking or feeling. Tracks will never again be just lifeless depressions in the ground. They bring the animal back to life, as it was in that point in time when it made the track.

In essence, what I am saying is that one can know an animal or human far better through the tracks it makes than by actually seeing that animal or human. I remember one of the many times I was able to illustrate this first-hand to a class. I was seated at the far side of a field at my school, lecturing to the students about sign tracking. In the distance I could hear the concentric ring of a moving fox, delivered by the alarm calls of various birds in the area. I watched the people's faces as the fox made its way into the center of the field and began to cross. My back was to the fox at the time, and I surprised most of the students when I told them that I wouldn't continue with the lecture until the fox was gone. This made them curious, for I had not turned to look.

After the concentric rings of disturbance faded in the distance and I knew the fox had exited the field, I asked the students a simple question. "Who knows that fox better," I asked, "you, who saw the fox, or me?" Knowing that my back had been to the fox, the class decided that they knew it better. With that I took them down to the tracks in the center of the field, glanced at the tracks momentarily, and put some questions to them. "Was the fox a male or female? To the ounce, how much did it weigh? Was its belly full or empty? Was it nervous, apprehensive, or confident in its travel across the field? Did it have any injury or sickness, or was it healthy?" On and on I went, asking question after question, with not one answer from my students. I then asked again, who knew the fox better. The answer was quite different this time around.

It is one thing to observe an animal in its travels, and quite another to read the tracks through the wisdom of the pressure releases. To merely observe the animal is to know very little about him. All observation does is identify the animal and learn a few of its habits. At best the typical observation scenario is quite short-lived, very superficial, and anticlimactic. To read the track is to have the animal frozen in time, where the track becomes a window not only to the past but to the animal's soul. Combine tracking with observation and you literally become the animal you are seeing. Tracking adds a tremendous depth to your understanding of the animal being tracked. Anything less is just superficial.

Exactly what is it I am looking at in a fox's track, you may be asking, that can tell me so much about the animal? At this point, since we are beginning where we should, with the science aspect of tracking, the answer is that I am looking at pressure releases—disturbances in the soil in and around the track. Some are quite large and easy to see, while others, at first, demand a closer inspection, usually from a prone position. It is best to imagine the track as being a miniature landscape, full of tiny hills, valleys, pocks, domes, ridges, waves, crests, crevasses, cracks, and many other features. You read the pressure releases of the track the same way that you would read a topographical map. In a way, the same forces that create our grander landscapes also work on the miniature landscapes of the track.

You will find that many of the names given to the pressure releases are those of geological formations. According to Grandfather, the Scouts would name a feature in a track after a similar feature they found on the larger landscape. For instance, the ridges and peaks in tracks are named for the ridges and peaks of mountain ranges that they resemble. Grandfather considered the Scouts to be among the earliest geologists. They knew the mechanics at work behind the pressure releases and understood that the same forces were behind the creation of the greater landscapes.

Young Scouts were taught the pressure releases through stories of giants who created the larger landscapes with their huge footprints. Although for the most part these stories were intended as teaching devices only, and were not part of the Apache creation story, they still held a tremendous power. Through them, the young Scout could clearly see the correlation between the grand landscapes and the landscapes of the track. Thus one would explain the other and the understanding encompassed both the minute and the magnificent. Grandfather often said that to understand the grander vistas of life we first must understand and appreciate the minute. I feel that this philosophy came directly through the teaching of the pressure releases.

The number of pressure releases are staggering, almost inconceivable.

In their sheer numbers, one can clearly see that they are not the work of just one person but of countless generations of Scouts. Grandfather feared that he was one of the last to possess this knowledge and that when he passed into spirit the wisdom of the pressure releases would probably be lost forever. I think that is why he taught me the wisdom of the pressure releases with such a passion. Often he would tell me that I would someday be responsible for keeping this wisdom alive. This concerned me as a child, but frightened me more as I grew older: I never met another tracker who possessed the wisdom of the pressure releases. That is why, for the past twenty years my school has been in operation, I have taught the pressure releases even in my most basic classes. It is also one of the major forces behind the writing of this difficult book. I do not want this knowledge to die.

Amazingly, over five thousand pressure releases have been identified. Surprisingly, I have only been able to add four new pressure releases to the list, and that is after nearly forty years of study. The numbers are staggering, yet when taken slowly, their organization is easily understood. Essentially there are two categories of pressure releases: the Major Pressure Release System and the Minor Pressure Release System. Unfortunately the latter system is far too involved to be covered in this book. The following is a breakdown of these two categories and the numbers of pressure releases found in each.

MAJOR PRESSURE RELEASES

Primaries	85
Secondaries	85
Externals	85
External Secondaries	85
Internals	85
Internal Secondaries	85
Indicators	65 minimum
Indicator Secondaries	65 minimum
Digitals	121
Digital Secondaries	121
Lobulars	146
Lobular Secondaries	146
Toe Ridges	182
Toe Ridge Secondaries	182

MINOR PRESSURE RELEASES

Macros	621
Macro Secondaries	621
Micros	1,686
Micro Secondaries	1,686

Considering the staggering number of pressure releases it is easy to see that it took generations of work to identify each one and to accumulate this knowledge. Keep in mind that each pressure release indicates a body function, a movement, or even a thought. These pressure releases, singularly or in combination, create a miniature landscape in each footprint.

A pressure release has nothing to do with the size of the animal, the weight of the animal, the shape of the foot, or even, in the case of the human animal, whether the foot has a shoe on it or not. Again, the pressure releases left by a galloping bear are identical to the pressure releases left by a galloping mouse, in proportion to its track. Pressure releases are not made by any distinct feature of the foot or by how the ground reacts to the pressure of the foot. Thus all pressure releases are the same for any given movement. It makes no difference what animal, even a human, is making that movement; the earth will react the same way.

The first photograph is a footprint in damp sand. This footprint is called a *stamp* because I simply placed my foot on the ground then added my weight. I did not move in any direction other than to apply and remove pressure. Unfortunately, this is all most people see when they look at a track. Essentially it is a dead track, meaning that it has no motion or flex.

In the following photo I have added the natural motion of moving forward. At this point in the series of tracks I made, I was accelerating from a walk to a jog. You will note that a large, disk-shaped pressure release appears, beginning at the center of the foot's ball and terminating at its center arch. This is one of the many pressure releases dealing with forward motion. No physical characteristic of my foot created this—just the pressure of an object pushing back against the soil to accelerate forward motion.

As I said before, a pressure release has nothing to do with weight, the size of the foot, shape of the foot, or any other physical characteristic of the foot or shoe. The following three photographs illustrate this. (See page 46.) In photo 3 you will note that I created the same pressure

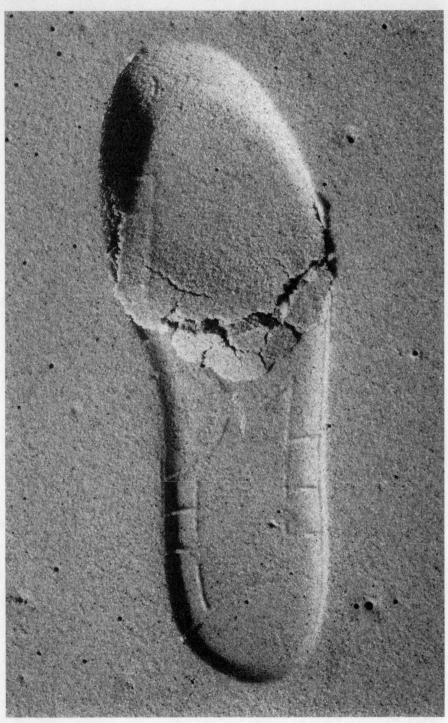

2

release using a block of wood. In photo 4 I created the same pressure release with my hand, and in photo 5 you will note the same pressure release in this animal track. Though the agent that formed each of these three tracks is different—a block of wood, my hand, and an animal's paw—the pressure shift was the same, thus the pressure release was the same. This is what I mean when I say a galloping bear will leave the same pressure releases as a galloping mouse.

This is very obvious in damp sand, you are probably saying, but in the real world we rarely encounter such perfect conditions. This is true, but remember that the principles behind pressure releases are the same regardless of the conditions. The best illustrations are found in damp sand, so that's the best place to start learning pressure releases. We call damp sand *zero earth* (or *zero soil*), and it is the easiest place to see, and thus learn, the tracks. Once you've understood and mastered tracking in zero earth, you can graduate to the more difficult tracking conditions. Even onto solid rock. Yes, the pressure releases even occur on solid rock, and on floors, as well as in every other tracking environment.

Although the principles do not vary, it is true that soil types, soil conditions, soil adhesive qualities, and many other factors determine the ultimate shape of the pressure releases. In damp sand a pressure release will be well defined and have very clean edges, while in dry sand the same pressure release will be a bit more rounded with soft edges. You will note in photograph 6, the clean, disk-shaped pressure release made in damp sand, while the same pressure release in photo 7, made in dry sand, has softer edges. All of these slight soil variations and conditions will be thoroughly discussed in chapter 13. Before we discuss these variations you need a broad and firm foundation in pressure releases as well as a little dirt time, meaning real experience.

BUILDING A TRACKING BOX

The importance of learning pressure releases first in damp sand cannot be stressed enough at this point. Because of this, I recommend to my students that they build a tracking box for the purpose. Even with the sugar-sand trails of the Pine Barrens right outside my door, as a child I also built a tracking box in my basement. This way, no matter what the weather conditions or time of day, I could just go down into my basement and keep tracking. Even though you will easily graduate from the sand-filled tracking box to the more difficult tracking environments within six months to a year, depending on your practice time, you will still come back to the tracking box to further refine your tracking skills. It is not something that you will use only once and then abandon.

If you are limited for space you can build a smaller tracking box, though I prefer a larger box, where you can take several complete steps without running out of box space. The ideal tracking box is eight feet long, four feet

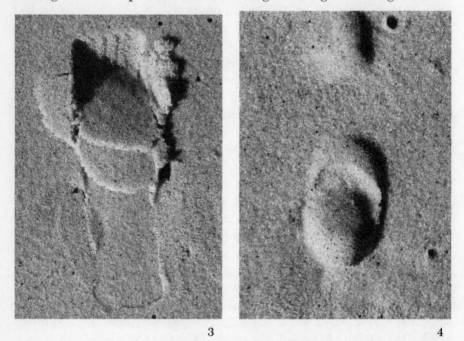

3

4

wide, and ten inches deep. I buy three two-by-tens that are eight feet long. I cut one board in half and hammer the four boards together so they form a rectangle. I make sure that the surface on which I place this rectangular frame is firm and flat. Most of my

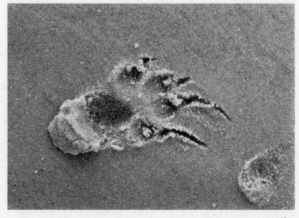

5

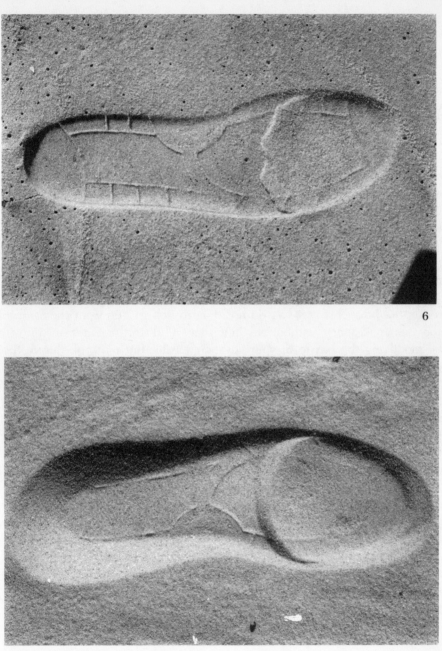

6

7

students put the box in the basement or garage. Some of them leave it outside for their children to play in when it's not being used as a tracking box. I have heard that some even keep it under the bed.

Once the box is in place, line the entire thing with a sheet of plastic and staple it into place. With the entire bottom and sides lined in plastic, you need not worry about putting a floor in the box. This plastic will keep the sand from seeping under the frame, and it will also keep the sand clean—and damp. Now fill the box up with sand to at least eight inches deep. Anything less tends not to allow enough buffer, and secondary pressure releases will be affected. You can obtain this pure granular sand from a cement company or, if pressed, you can buy children's play sand, the type used for children's sandboxes. Now dampen the sand with a spray of water until it's damp, not wet, then press it down and smooth it with a wide board. The box is now ready for use. However, when not in use make sure you cover the box, not only to keep it clean but also to keep in the moisture so that you do not have to wet the sand every time.

It is important to note that you should wipe your feet well before entering the box. This way you do not drag in debris. You want the sand to stay one consistency, without anything that will distort it. Later on you will be modifying the box to fit your advancing skills, but more on that in the next chapter.

Although I have had many good tracking students who never made a tracking box at all, who happened to live in a sandy environment already, I do recommend them strongly. Even if the box you build is only two feet by two feet, it will be of tremendous value. The nice thing about having the tracking box at your disposal when reading this book is that you can experiment right away and follow the text as you go.

Now that your tracking box is built or you have located a damp sandy area outside, you are ready to move forward. I feel that the best way to proceed is first to read this book thoroughly, which will build a firm foundation. Then take this book outside and put it to use, chapter by chapter, as a field guide. Once you understand the pressure releases in the damp sand, you will find yourself alternating between the tracking box and the more difficult tracking environments, in most cases right away.

In the next six chapters you will see the pressure releases come to life. We can attach meaning to each little formation found in the track and connect that meaning back to a movement or condition of that animal or person. The result of your work will be the preservation of a skill and knowledge that otherwise would have been lost to the modern world. You will become one of the grandchildren that carry this knowledge into the future, preserving it for your children and grandchildren.

6. PRESSURE AGAINST THE WALL

Our first pressure release study, called "pressure against the wall," will help you determine primarily whether the animal has shifted direction in even the slightest way. It can also show a loss of balance, shifts in body weight, extreme head turns, stopping or slowing, and several other smaller movements. Before we go on, however, it is important to go over some track nomenclature so that we can begin to speak a common language.

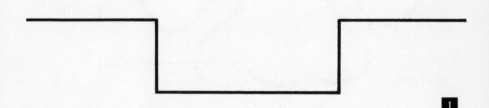

In illustration 1 I have drawn a cross-section of a stamp track. As you recall from photo 1 in chapter 5, natural tracks do not occur in this way, but when it comes to the way most people look at tracks, draw tracks, or measure tracks, this is what they see. In so doing, they usually see and measure the track incorrectly. Illustration 2 shows a cross-section of a track the way it is actually made. When moving forward, the foot strikes the ground at an angle, registers and spreads as weight is applied, then exits at an angle. Thus the track has sloping walls, which the illustration depicts. However, keep in mind that this cross-section is not necessarily drawn from

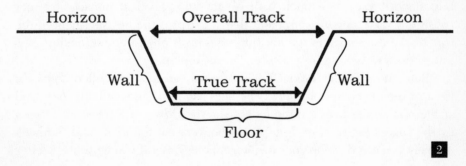

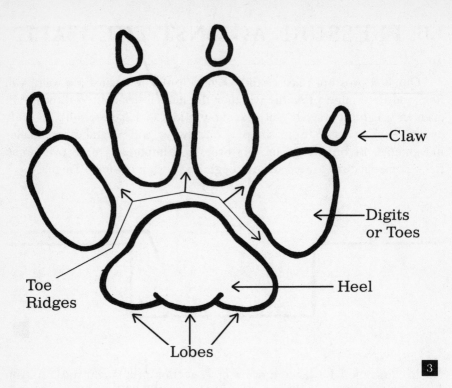

heel to toe; due to the spreading factor of the weighted foot, the track also spreads from side to side, giving it the same sloping appearance.

Ground level of the track is called the *horizon*, the sides of the track are called the *walls*, and the bottom of the track, the track *floor*. Where the wall meets the horizon is called the *horizon cut* and where the floor meets the wall is called the *lateral ridge*. Measuring or drawing the track using the *overall* track measurements (shown in the illustration) is common but, since it varies so much with weight and speed at impact, it is not consistent. The only measurement that I accept is the measurement of the *true* track (also shown in the illustration). This is often more difficult to see, but it tends to be a more consistent measurement.

Refer now to illustration 3. The toes of the foot are called *digits*. In front of the digits are the *claws*. The heel pad is called simply the *heel*, and at the rear of the heel are the *lobes*. The *toe ridges* of a track are formed by the spaces between each digit and between all the digits and the heel. Actually you can develop your own terminology, but if you write me a letter

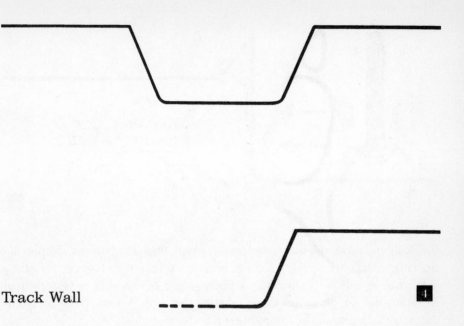

Track Wall   4

or come to my classes, please use these terms. I have been using these terms since I was a child and old habits tend to be hard to break. Basically I have been trying to develop a more universal language for trackers where there has been none before, and with well over twenty thousand graduates of my school, I have a fairly good start. So please use them so we speak a common tongue.

Let's now get into the study of pressure against the wall. Remember, the walls of the track run all the way around. These walls are not only found on the sides of the track but also in the toe and heel areas. Note, too, that track walls are found even on hard surfaces, such as solid rock faces and floors, as well as in every other conceivable tracking environment. Refer now to illustration 4, a cross-section of a track wall. I have drawn it this way so that you do not get the idea that this is any one particular part of the track, such as the side, toe, or heel area. Instead, by seeing it depicted in this manner, you will remember that this pressure can appear on any wall.

Illustration 5 shows the foot's effects on the wall of the track. It starts with down arrow, where the foot is planted firmly in the soil. Once planted, the foot presses up against the wall and buckles the wall. The wall and horizon of the track are thus affected and this is where the pressure against

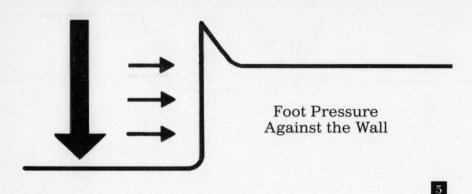

Foot Pressure
Against the Wall

5

the wall pressure releases are found. I will use this type of simple line drawing to show the progression of pressure releases throughout the study. Wherever it will help I include a photograph; however, it is very difficult to show some of these pressure releases that way. Where possible I have cut into the track and photographed the cross-section.

The Cliff

The first pressure release is called a *cliff*. Referring to illustration 6, you will see that the wall of the track looks unaffected, and you are right. Anytime you see a wall like this it means that the foot went straight in and out at this point, never applying any pressure against the wall, other than the initial spread of the foot. Now you are probably asking yourself what more does this "cliff" mean, other than having no pressure exerted on the wall. I will answer that question a little later in the text. I first want to build on these first few pressure releases, make sure you have a firm understanding of the process, then go on to explain the pressure in detail.

The Cliff

6

The Ridge

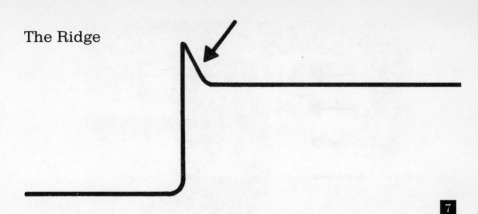

7

The Ridge

In illustration 7, you can clearly see a ridge rising above the horizon of the track. This means that after the foot was planted in the ground it pressed lightly on the wall of the track. The pressure buckled the wall, which forced the ridge upward, beyond the horizon of the track. How much pressure? you may ask. Imagine that you are standing still with one foot ahead of the other, as if you'd been walking and come to a stop. Imagine now that sticking out from your chest is the hour hand of a huge clock, and you are facing

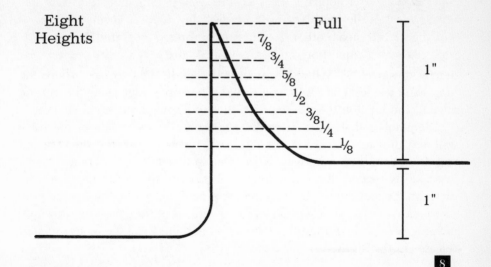

8

8

exactly toward 12:00. Now if you turned slightly right to face where the hour hand would be at 12:15, you would throw up a ridge along the outside edge of the heel on the leading foot, thus indicating a direction change.

Remember that these line drawings show a cross-section of the track wall and pressure release. You can clearly see how high the ridge is, but you do not see how long it is. Now refer to illustration 8. A ridge can be just a thirty-second of an inch long or it can run the entire length of the footprint, depending on the amount of pressure placed on the foot and the surface area involved. Keep this in mind with all of the following drawings, for what holds true of the ridge length also pertains to all the other pressure releases in this study.

The Peak

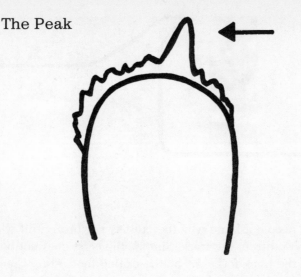

9

The Peak

A peak is the highest point on a ridge, indicating the place of highest pressure. Refer now to illustration 9. For simplicity's sake let's say that a human, wearing shoes, came to a stop. You will note that a ridge has been thrown up on the toe area of the track. Above the ridge is a higher projection and that projection is the Peak. The peak indicates the point of highest pressure along a ridge, and, as you can see from the illustration, the highest pressure in this case was not in the center but off to the side. This simply means that the human shifted slightly to the right as he or she stopped. A peak can stand alone; this would depict a place of abrupt, pinpoint pressure in a given track.

The Crest

By applying more pressure and added intensity to the track, the ridge rises upward, then bends back toward the center of the track slightly (see illustration 10). The result is a *crest*. By "added intensity," I mean that the foot bumped the wall slightly before it added pressure. It is the difference between placing your hands on an object, then pushing, and moving your hands quickly toward the object, hitting the object, then pushing. It is not as abrupt as it may sound, though. The *intensity* is simply a little more of a shock wave added to an existing pressure.

The Crest

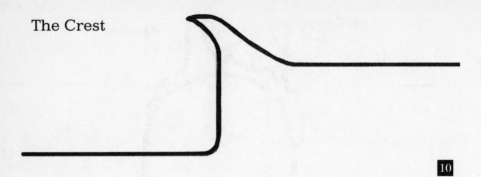

10

Many people ask me why the crest is not broken off when the foot is being removed from the track. Simply, the crest does not bend far enough back over the track to be hit by the exiting foot. Also, when the weight is removed from the foot, the foot shrinks and easily passes the crest without hitting it. A foot is narrow until weight is put on it, then it spreads; when the weight is removed, it shrinks and becomes narrower. These two factors—the lean of the crest and foot shrinkage—rarely allow the foot to hit the crest upon exiting. I say "rarely," for sometimes it does hit the crest, and this we call a *distortion*. I'll talk more about track distortion later in this chapter.

What would cause a crest? Imagine again that you are standing on that clock. If you change direction from 12:00 to 12:15 you will throw a ridge. If you go farther, say to 12:30, you will throw a crest. Remember that this pressure release study is ever increasing in pressure as we go. We began with no pressure against the wall, which was a cliff, then we added a little pressure and threw a ridge, more specific pressure made a peak, and more pressure and intensity gave us a crest.

The Crest-Crumble
Now let's say you are part of that clock again and you turn from 12:00 to 12:45. You will create on the outside of the heel what is called a *crest-crumble* (see illustration 11). You will note that the wall was hit with such pressure and intensity that the shock waves caused the crest to break apart and fall into the track. Considering that you are only changing direction from 12:00 to 12:45, this is not as much pressure and intensity as it may sound like. In fact, all of the pressure releases to this point are considered to be just light pressure against the wall.

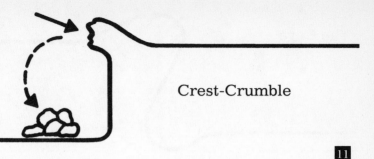

Crest-Crumble

11

Please particularly note that I am hyphenating this term, *crest-crumble*. Consider the fact that there are over five thousand pressure releases and just so many words of description. In addition, we have to show correlation between pressure releases. Hyphens—or the absence of hyphens—are extremely important for distinguishing between closely related terms. For instance, there is a crest-crumble, a crest crumble, and a crestcrumble. Each is different. Whenever I convey information in the field to other trackers via either radio or courier, I make very sure they know which of the "crest crumbles" I am talking about. Yet it's a simple distinction, and you'll see the pattern repeated through the entire book. A *crest-crumble*, as you know, means more pressure against the wall than in a crest. A *crest crumble* is a crest that has crumbled long after the foot left the track. This crumbling is due to the action of the weather. Finally, a *crestcrumble* is just a crest that has crumbled because the foot hit it upon exiting the track.

You might be asking yourself how you will ever know the difference between all of these "crest crumbles." Well, the answer is dirt time. How much dirt time? Oh, I'd say about four hours' worth. Probably much less, for it is very easy to see the difference in these tracks. In a crest-crumble, the age of the crumbled crest is the same as the age of the rest of the track. In a crest crumble, the age of the crumbled crest is much younger than the rest of the track. And in the crestcrumble, the crumbling is scattered and the track damaged. After all, the exiting foot did have to hit the crest to cause it to crumble.

The Cave

Now we move into higher and more intense pressure against the wall, caused by more dramatic turns. This and the next pressure release are nonetheless only considered to be moderate pressure against the wall. What happens here is a slight bending down of the foot, actually digging in under the wall (see il-

The Cave

12

lustration 12). Try this experiment: Place your foot flat and firm on the ground with equal weight on ball and heel. Now pivot your foot on the ball as if you were making a turn to the right or left. What you will feel is a grabbing of the ground and a downward driving motion of the foot. To imagine this on that clock again, it is like changing direction from 12:00 to 1:00.

The Cave-in

Why not a cave-crumble? Well, because one of the macro pressure releases (which are beyond the scope of this book) is called a cave-crumble. So for this larger pressure release we add -*in* instead of -*crumble*. Using that imaginary clock again, you are changing direction from 12:00 to 1:15 and even beyond. Certainly a more dramatic turn. Here again we have a cave-in, a cave in, and a cavein—all with the same differences as before. The cave-in is caused by higher pressure than the cave. A cave in results from the weathering of the track. And the cavein happens when the foot hits the track upon exiting. See illustration 13.

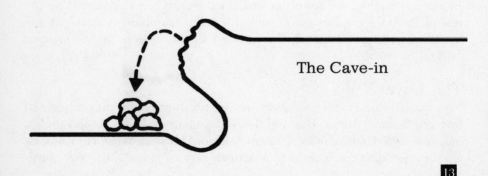

The Cave-in

13

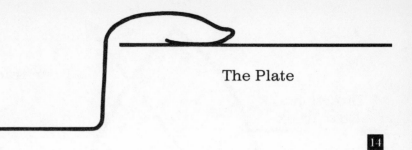

The Plate

14

The Plate

This is the first of the pressure releases caused by what is considered very high pressure against the wall. These depict very dramatic turns and stops, which overpressurize the wall with tremendous intensity. We have gone into the wall as far as we can go, down into the track as far as we can go, and there is but one place left for the pressure to go. The pressure has to go up. What happens with this wall is that it buckles under the strain, splits far back on the horizon, and a huge platelike disk of earth slides high up on the horizon. See illustration 14 and photo 9.

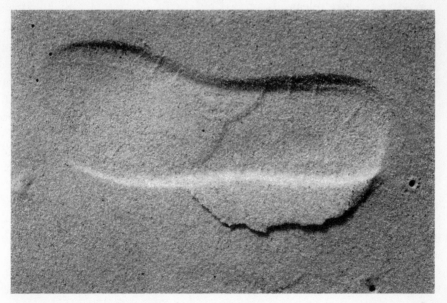

9

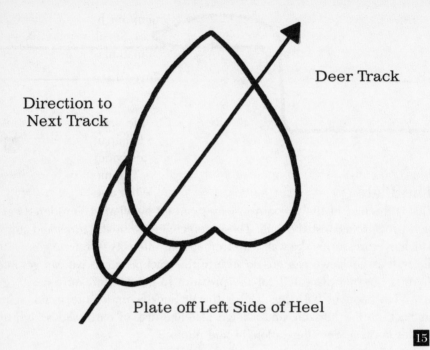

Direction to
Next Track

Deer Track

Plate off Left Side of Heel

15

Besides telling you everything about an animal, the pressure releases will tell you exactly where you will find the next track before you even see it. Once you become a master tracker it will be almost impossible for you to lose a trail. Grandfather said, "All the wisdom lies in the last track." What he meant by that is that if read properly, the track at hand will tell you everything about the next track, including its location. Notice in illustration 15 and in photo 10 that there is a plate coming off the outside of the heel of the track. A line drawn through the plate, dividing it equally in half, will point directly to the next track.

The Plate-Fissure

You guessed it. As soon as we add more intensity and pressure to the plate it begins to fissure. I am purposely not saying "it begins to *crack*" because we use the word *crack* to describe what happens when ground dries out. Cracking has nothing to do with track wall pressure. That is why we call this a *fissure*, for fissures have everything to do with pressure. As it is caused by a more dramatic turn, the hyphenation is important here for the same reasons it is important to the other pressure releases. See illustration 16 and photo 11. Fissuring tends to occur through a combination of added pressure and intensity but more so with the intensity.

The Plate-Crumble

Now with more pressure and intensity added to the wall and the existing plate-fissure, it fractures even more and begins to fall apart (see illustration 17 and photo 12). During its formation the fissures widen, fracture like a mosaic, and then finally crumble around the edges. The more extreme pressures will cause not only the outer edge to crumble but also the entire plate. Again I must state that the hyphen here is important when conveying any information into your notes, letters, or to other trackers.

10

Plate-Fissure

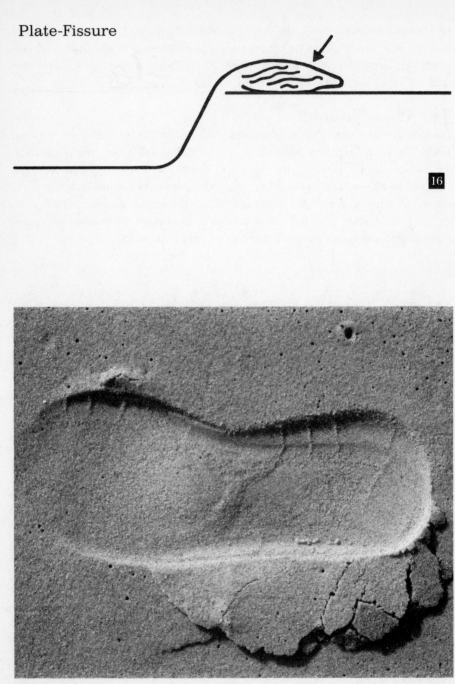

16

11

Plate-Crumble

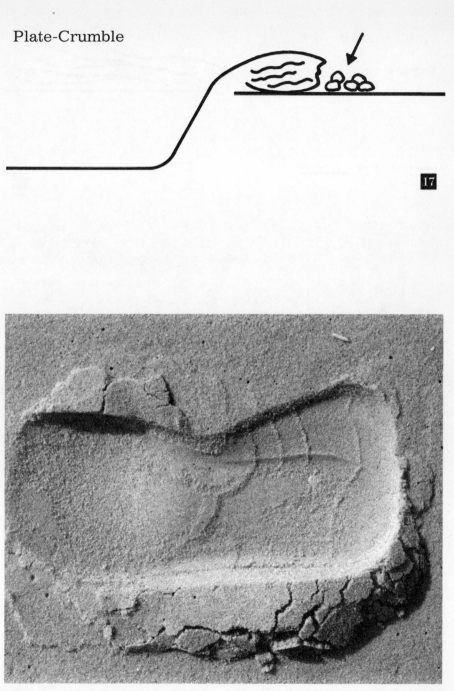

17

12

Explosion

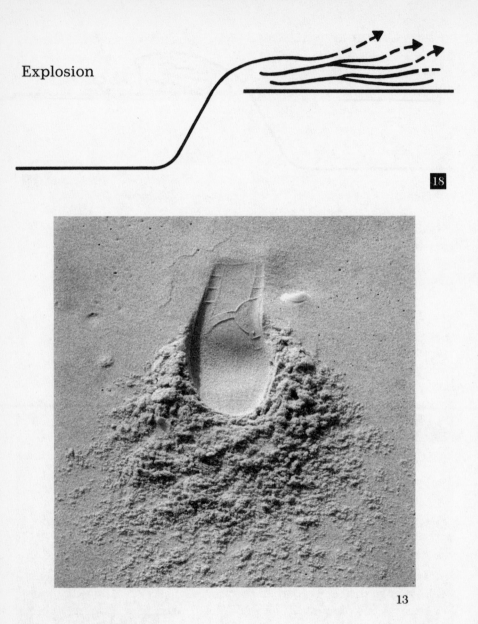

18

13

The Explosion

Here we have the extreme in wall pressure. The wall is essentially hit with such violent pressure and intensity that it literally explodes, or blows soil outward. Depending on the pressure and intensity involved, it can fan dirt several feet out from the track. See illustration 18 and photo 13. Here we have the most extreme turns and stops. These explosions do not occur only when the animal or human is moving quickly; they can also happen when moving slowly. The speed of the forward motion makes no difference, for this pressure release originates in the power of the turn or the stop.

It is important to remind you that these pressure releases are a progression of pressure. For instance, let's say that you kick the ground hard with your foot, spewing dirt far in front of the track in a dramatic explosion. If you were to videotape the process and play it back in slow motion you would find that the explosion begins with a cliff, moves to a ridge, then a peak, then a crest, then a crest-crumble, into a cave, then to a cave-in, then rising up from the ground comes a plate, a plate-fissure, a plate-crumble, then finally the ensuing explosion.

Measuring the Eights

On a more advanced note, there are not just eleven primary pressure releases in this study, but nearly ten times that many. In order to keep this book simple and understandable I have had to leave out many definitive pressure releases that fit into this category. They are basically the same pressure releases that you have learned. The only difference is that they come in sizes. For instance, there are eight sizes of cliffs, ridges, peaks, crests, crest-crumbles, caves, cave-ins, plates, plate-fissures, plate-crumbles, and explosions. In other words, the taller the ridge or crest, or the wider and longer the plate, the more pressure and intensity was exerted. These are usually noted in proportion to the track.

I said that ridges, to use those for an example, come in eight different sizes. A ridge that is as high as the track is deep is called a full ridge. A ridge half as high as the track is deep is called a half ridge, a quarter the size as the track is deep is called a quarter ridge, and so on. Using this track depth to ridge height proportion you can have an eighth ridge, indicating low pressure and intensity. Then with ever-increasing pressure and intensity you can move to a quarter ridge, a three-eighths ridge, a half ridge, and so on. They are all still called ridges, but the increments allow for precise measurement of pressure (see illustration 8, page 55).

This process of dividing all these wall pressure releases into increments is not important to you right now. As I stated, I want to keep it simple. I know, however, that soon you will begin to note the various sizes of these pressure releases as you practice. Knowing this clue—that all pressure releases are measured in increments called *eights*—you can figure out the meanings of the various sizes with ease. Once again think about facing 12:00 o'clock. I originally told you that a ridge is thrown when you change directions from 12:00 to 12:15. The different numbers of eights would be thrown at all the smaller direction shifts in between 12:00 and 12:15. For instance, a half ridge would be thrown when you turned to 12:07.

Chapter 15 is devoted to a fuller discussion of the eights increments.

PRIMARY AND SECONDARY PRESSURE RELEASES

As you are probably beginning to see at this point, the system is a bit more complicated than just the basic eleven pressure against the wall pressure releases we have been discussing thus far. Not only are these pressure releases further distinguished by size, but when pressure releases begin to ride upon other pressure releases, these "riders" are called *secondary* pressure releases. The ones you have learned thus far are called *primary* pressure releases. This means that they indicate a major movement, such as a turn or stop. If they stood alone it would all be so simple, but they rarely stand alone. We are not machines, nor are other animals machines. We do not move in a smooth, robotic fashion. Instead, we are constantly struggling to stay upright against the forces of gravity, balance, wind resistance, topographical changes, friction, and many other factors.

Given that all these outside influences are constantly at work against us, our motions are rarely fluid. What may feel like a smooth turn to the right when you are observing an animal usually isn't smooth at all. This becomes evident when you look into your track and see the shape and numbers of pressure releases involved in just that one simple turn. You will see the primaries, which show the primary movement, but you will also see the secondary pressure releases riding upon them, showing a secondary motion or effort. Rarely will you find a primary standing alone; instead, you will probably have a primary with several secondaries.

In illustration 19, you will see a primary plate-fissure. Because of its size and its place on the pressure scale, this is the pressure release that depicts the major motion. You will also note that there are three other pressure releases riding on or alongside the primary. You will note the crest, the cave, and a plate. What this shows is that you have a primary motion fol-

Secondaries

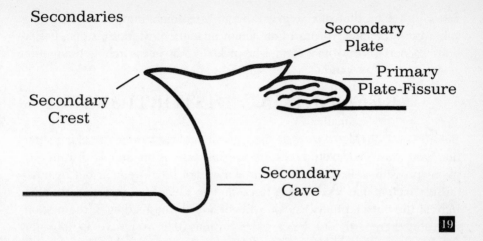

Secondary
Plate

Primary
Plate-Fissure

Secondary
Crest

Secondary
Cave

19

lowed by three secondary motions, all coming together to complete the final movement. What this also tells you is that the motion was not smooth, but consisted of four separate but linked motions. To explain this further let's use an example. Imagine that you are watching someone walking along a trail. Suddenly he stops, turns around in his tracks, and looks at the ground beside him, as if he dropped something. It may appear to be one smooth motion, but probably not.

You now go over and look at the tracks that the man made when he stopped to look at the ground. On the outside of the heel you see a primary plate-fissure, with a secondary plate, a secondary crest, and a secondary cave. Now you know it was not a smooth motion. Instead, much of the turnaround was registered as the primary plate-fissure. But then there was a momentary pause, imperceptible to the eye—perhaps a thought—and then the turning motion continued a bit further, thus throwing the second plate. Another slight pause and the head turned partially downward, throwing the cave. Then finally another slight imperceptible pause and the head looks at the ground, throwing the crest. These secondaries are the rule and not the exception.

Essentially, the eleven primary pressure releases you learned show up again as secondaries. Secondaries ride upon primaries. So now you understand eleven primary pressure releases and eleven secondaries. Not so simple, however, for secondaries, like the primaries, are divided into eights. Yes, secondaries are measured in increments just like the larger primaries, and for the same reason. Though the secondaries may seem complicated at first and a source of distraction, they are extremely important. They give you a more defined picture of an action or motion. Motions, stops, hesitations, second efforts—that cannot be picked up by just watching the motion alone.

RECOGNIZING DISTORTIONS

Before you even begin to read the pressure releases in any tracking situation, you must first look for distortions. Distortions are simply distorted or phony pressure releases that are thrown up not by movement but by other outside factors and forces. It is important to identify a distortion situation right at the outset, otherwise you will get a distorted reading of the motion. Basically there are four types of distortions that you have to look out for. You have already learned two of them. A crest crumble is a *weather-imposed* distortion—meaning that the pressure release was originally a crest but, due to the action of the weather, it crumbled. The other distortion you know is a *self-imposed* distortion. That is where the foot, upon exiting the track, hits the pressure release and distorts it, as in a crestcrumble. A *mechanical-imposed* distortion usually only applies to humans with shoes on, where some feature of the shoe causes a phony pressure release to be thrown. See photo 14. For instance, if the sole of the shoe has a flare, it will undercut the wall, thus throwing a mechanical-imposed distortion with the flared sole. Someone not aware of these mechanical distortions may wrongly interpret it as a cave.

The most common distortion is called a *landscape-imposed* distortion. This is where topography or debris imbedded in the soil causes a phony pressure release to occur. In photo 15 we can see the huge plates thrown to the outside of the foot when walking across a hill. The slipping of the foot on the slope causes a phony plate to erupt. This has nothing to do with the human's intended motion but is caused by the condition of the landscape the person is walking upon. By far, these landscape-imposed distortions are some of the most difficult to detect. Defects on and beneath the soil can be obscure to the untrained eye. For instance, a small stone buried beneath the surface of the track floor can cause the foot to slide and turn, and if you know the stone is there, you will not misread the results in the track.

14

USING YOUR TRACKING BOX

It is now that the power of the tracking box will come into play. Using the box, you will find that with one hour of practice you will have a full understanding of the primary pressure releases, and within two hours you will have a firm handle on the whole pressure against the wall study. Many of my students tell me that through the tracking box they were able to master pressure release studies 1, 2, and 3 within four hours. The importance of the tracking box cannot be stressed enough at this point.

To use the tracking box, take several steps through the box, turning right, then left, then looking down, then slowing, and so on. Remember what you have done. Some students make mental notes of the process, while others, carrying a tape recorder, give an ongoing description of what they are doing, and some even set up a video camera to record the motions. You

15

would be surprised how much you can forget once the motion is made. Now go back to the tracks and, remembering what you did for each, read the pressure releases. Each track will record your every movement on both a primary and secondary level. The nice thing about this process is that you know what you did in the motion and now you can back it up with the pressure releases.

Once you have used the tracking box for four to six hours, it is time to test your skill. Have another person walk through the box when your back is turned. Now, once the tracks are set down, begin reading the pressure releases and tell your friend what he or she has done. Both of you will be shocked by how much you will be able to tell about their walk. I suggest you have an unbiased onlooker or a video camera for this one to prevent arguments. You may see a pressure release, for instance, that tells you that your friend has slightly lost his balance, which he probably won't remember.

Generally people don't pay attention to the little nuances of their walk—
nuances that are glaringly apparent in the tracks. This way there are no
arguments.

Pressure against the wall will show any slight direction change an animal
or human makes. It will also show slowing or stopping, as well as many
other smaller motions, like loss of balance, head turning, and bending motions. The pressure on the wall, and the intensity with which that pressure
is delivered, will produce a vast array of pressure releases. These increments
of pressure show precise movements and secondary motions. Understanding
this pressure release study allows us to read direction change in a track.
Now we move on to the next pressure release study, which illustrates the
signs of forward motion.

7. CHANGING OR MAINTAINING FORWARD MOTION

Hopefully you have worked a little in your tracking box before you got to this point, but it's not really essential. Especially if you are reading through the book once first, planning to go back through the material later as you log some dirt time. When teaching my classes, I have found that taking the students to the tracking box after each pressure release study is completed tends to be far more effective than delivering all the lectures first and then going to the box. They get a full understanding of the process as they go along; a feel right away for how the soil moves. Understanding this initial movement and reaction process makes all the other studies that much easier. For the reader, however, the photographs should allow you to move right through the text and understand the concepts without having to go to the tracking box.

Grandfather said, "All soil moves in the same way." Soil, dirt, the earth—under the influence of track pressure, all will move in virtually the same way, no matter what other influences or what motions the track dictates. Thus, understanding basic soil movement principles can greatly enhance your understanding of all pressure release studies. You will see the magic of these soil movement principles take place in this pressure release study, and it will become more dramatic when we get to pressure release studies 4, 5, and 6. However, all you have to remember for now is that all dirt moves in much the same way.

This study deals with the changing or maintaining of forward motion. As each pressure release of motion unfolds, I will correlate that pressure release to the movements and speed of both animal and human. A lot of dynamics of pressure, intensity of pressure, and surface area are involved in forward motion pressure releases; I will discuss these as we go along. But for right now I must stress an important concept. I said earlier that a galloping bear would leave the exact same pressure releases as a galloping mouse. The pressure releases are virtually the same—even though they are not moving forward at the same speed. This is because the surface area of the bear's foot in proportion to the size and weight of its body is virtually the same as the mouse's foot in proportion to its body. Given that equal proportionality, it takes the same effort from both bear and mouse to reach gallop speed, thus the intensity and pressure affect the soil in the same way. That is why the pressure releases that indicate relative speed of the animal—that indicate whether it is moving at a gallop, bound, trot, or walk,

The Wave

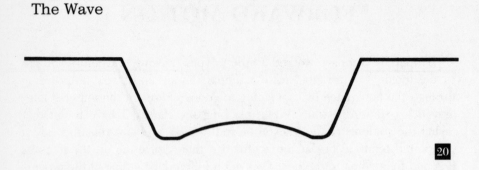

20

for example—are the same for every animal. Actual speed (in miles per hour) is then the only thing that varies.

In the line drawing illustrations accompanying this study, I have drawn the tracks in cross-section from heel to toe, as if the animal or human were walking across the page from left to right. The heel enters from the left, registers the track, then exits at the toe to the right. As we go through this study we will be using a human foot for illustration and photographs. This is only because the human foot initially throws more dramatic pressure releases. In the latter section of the book will be numerous photographs of pressure releases in animal tracks.

The Wave
Here in the first increment of forward motion, the heel strikes the ground at an angle, forcing a mound of earth up in front. The foot now rolls over the mound, compressing the earth, then presses on the front of the mound to gain forward motion. Remember that in order to move forward there must be a pushing-off motion—in other words, an equal and opposite reaction. This mound is called a wave (see illustration 20). Whenever you see this in a human track, the human is slow walking or strolling. When seen in any animal track, it is a slow walk. Slow walk is defined as wandering without real purpose or hurry, slower than the normal walk.

The Double Wave
In order to go faster, the human or animal must push off harder, thus building on the original wave. It is important to keep in mind here that

The Double Wave

21

when I refer to the "mound of earth" or the "wave," it is not as big and dramatic as it may sound. It is more of a slight mounding or rolling of the track floor. Here the heel enters the ground again and rolls over the mound, but now there is a little more effort and intensity in the pushing off. The front of the original wave buckles slightly from toe action and produces a second, smaller wave on the nose of the original (see illustration 21). This pressure release is called a double wave, and in both animal or human tracks it means a natural walk. Walking is defined as going to a place with a purpose.

The Disk

As the animal or human now picks up in speed, something very dynamic begins to happen to the soil. Essentially the foot hits and compresses the initial wave in the same way, but to go faster it adds more pressure and intensity. Here the toes and ball of the foot press hard against the wave, fracturing off a disk-shaped clump of soil at the front of the wave (see illustration 22 and photo 17). This pressure release is called a disk, and in

The Disk

22

17

both animal and human tracks it means a fast walk. Again, the shattering
of the front of the wave and the ensuing disk are a result of increased
pressure, thus a faster speed.

The Disk-Fissure

Moving faster still, the disk is formed in the same way, but, with the added
pressure and intensity, the disk fissures. Recall now the statement "All soil
moves in the same way." You will have noted that the disk has many of the
characteristics of the plate studied in the last chapter. Yes, it is nearly the
same and will react the same to pressure—i.e., it will fissure and eventually
crumble in this pressure for the same reasons as in the last pressure release
study. A disk fissure is weather-induced, and a diskfissure is self-induced.
Whenever you see a disk-fissure in a human track it means a slow jog and
in an animal track it indicates a trot. See illustration 23 and photo 18.

Disk-Fissure

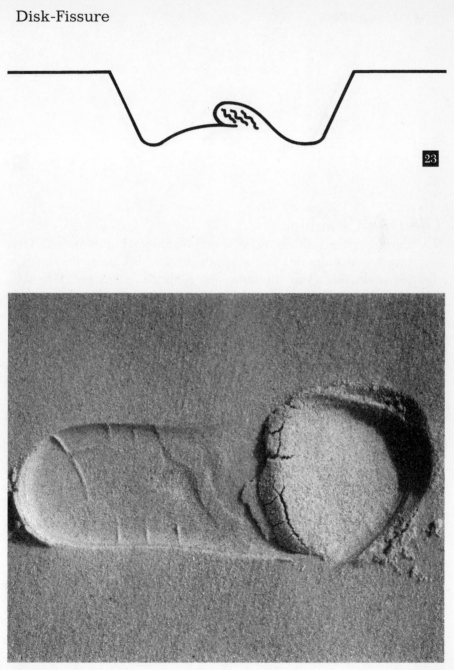

23

18

Disk-Crumble

The Disk-Crumble

Now moving faster again we need more pressure and intensity still. Here in this track (see illustration 24 and photo 19). The disk arises, fissures, then crumbles, indicating a harder pushing off and thus a faster speed. Whenever you see this in a human track it means a jog; in an animal track it is a fast trot.

The Dish

Now something even more dramatic happens to the track. As the animal or human picks up speed, more pressure, intensity, and surface area of the track are involved. The entire wave at this point sheers off and creates a large disk-shaped plate. This pressure release is called a dish. In a human track this pressure release indicates a fast jog, and in an animal's it indicates a bound. See illustration 25 and photo 20.

You might now be asking yourself when a disk becomes a dish. Actually the line between the disk and dish is quite definitive and very easy to spot, but I have to put that question off until later in the chapter, after I am done laying out the initial information. So just bear with me for a few more pressure releases.

The Dish-Fissure

Here again, the dish reacts like the disk, which reacts like the plate. It will fissure, then crumble, as more pressure and intensity are applied. The initial track is formed in the same way as the dish, but with the added intensity and pressure the dish is forced to fissure under stress (see illustration 26 and photo 21). This dish-fissure in a human track indicates a slow run and when found in an animal track it indicates a lope.

The Dish-Crumble

Add more pressure, intensity, and affected surface area and the dish falls apart. This is called a dish-crumble (see illustration 27 and photo 22). When seen in a human track this pressure release indicates a full run and in an animal's it means a gallop.

The Explode-Off

Finally, the pushing-off pressure and intensity of the movement far exceeds the surface area of the foot. The track blows out and scatters earth well beyond the heel print. See illustration 28 and photo 23. When seen in both human and animal tracks it means a sprint. I know you are probably wondering about the hyphen in this word. It actually does not follow the rule of the other hyphenated words, but has to do with something else entirely.

The Dish

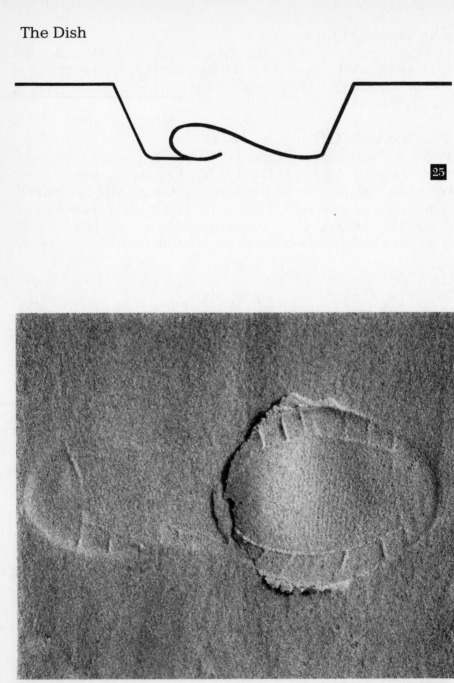

The Dish-Fissure

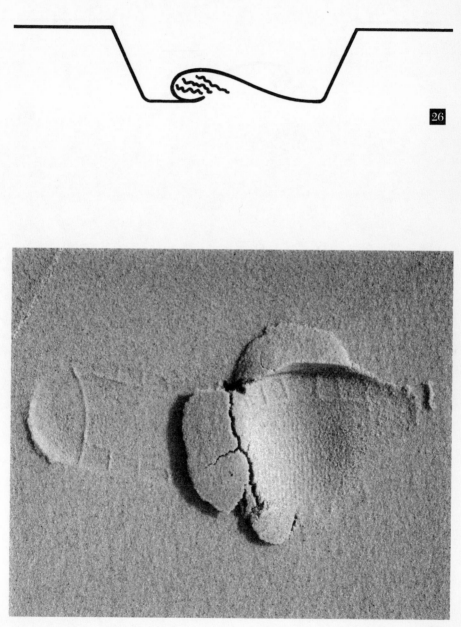

26

21

The Dish-Crumble

The Explode-Off

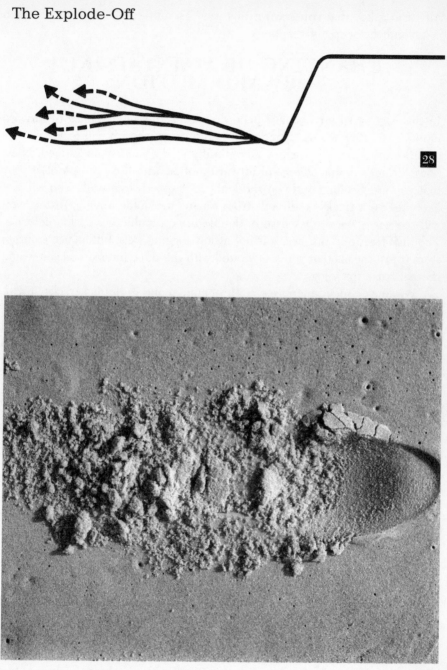

28

23

All I can ask is that you learn it this way. The difference with this hyphen is beyond the scope of this book.

CHANGING OR MAINTAINING
FORWARD MOTION

In this section so far we have been discussing the *maintenance* of forward motion. In other words, a human jogging along a beach will leave a series of disk-crumbles, which show a continuity in the motion and speed. Now, however, let's define *change* of forward motion with this example. Let's say that you are strolling and you suddenly shift speeds to a walk. You will not likely see your tracks go directly from waving to double waving. Instead you will see wave, wave, disk-fissure, double wave, double wave, double wave. The disk-fissure in this series is not a slow jogging step, but an acceleration step. It just means that you accelerated with the same intensity as you would normally use for a jog.

Whenever speed increases, both in animal and in human tracks, it usually creates an acceleration step, or two, or more, depending on the conditions and how intense the change in speed. You will also find acceleration-like steps anytime an animal or human is going up a steep incline. The extra surface area and pressure in this case are needed to push the body up the incline. Here is where experience comes into play. If someone is jogging up a hill you will probably not find disk-fissures but something more like dish-fissures. The steepness of the grade and personality of the soil has much to do with what will be thrown. When I discuss soil personality later in the book this will make more sense to you.

Having defined the changing and maintaining of forward motion, we now arrive at the distinction between the disk and the dish. As I stated earlier, the line that divides them is very definitive and easy to identify. As you can see in illustration 29a, the dividing line between the disk area and the dish area is located at the rear of the foot's ball. The line actually touches the ball. Anything from the toe of the foot to that line is defined as a disk. Anything from that line to the heel is defined as a dish. Illustration 29b shows a deer hoof. Here the line simply cuts the track in two equal halves. Again, from the tip of the toes to that dividing line is the place of disks and from the dividing line into the heel is the place of dishes.

In an animal track, such as this cat print, which has a heel pad and toes, the dividing line becomes a bit more difficult to define. Referring now to illustration 29c, note the line that just touches the back of the center two

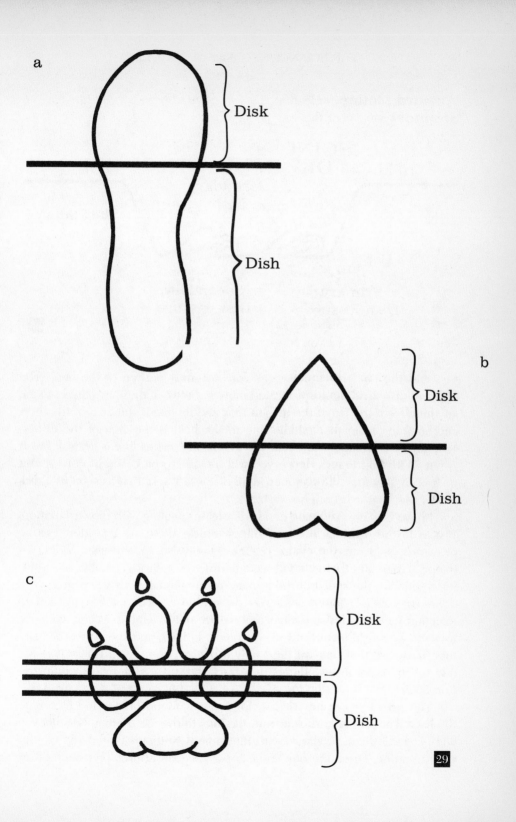

a

Disk

Dish

b

Disk

Dish

c

Disk

Dish

29

Forward Motion
Secondaries

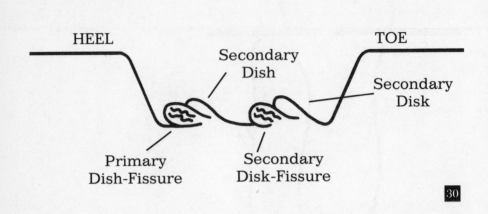

HEEL   TOE

Secondary
Dish

Secondary
Disk

Primary   Secondary
Dish-Fissure   Disk-Fissure

30

toes and the line that touches the forward-most portion of the heel. The
disk and dish dividing line is located midway between these two lines. Again,
anything from the tip of the toes to that middle line is the area of the disks
and anything from that middle line to the heel is the area of the dishes.
You may be imagining now that the measuring of this line is critical, but it
is not. With a little experience you will be able to pick it right out without
measuring any lines. Remember in all of these tracks that as soon as a disk
passes that line it becomes a dish.

I have now covered nine pressure releases dealing with forward motion.
Just as in the previous pressure release study, these are considered to be
primaries, or primary pressure releases. They also appear again, riding on
the primaries, and these we call secondaries. Secondaries actually have nothing to do with the speed of the human or the animal. Only the primary will
define the speed. The secondaries determine a second effort needed to
maintain that speed. Remember that we are not machines. When we move
forward we battle terrain, wind resistance, fatigue, and so many other factors. It is rare that you will find only a primary in a given track. It is not
odd to find several secondaries in a track, however. Refer now to illustration 30.

The primary pressure release for forward motion is located closest to
the heel. The secondaries run from the heel to the toe. Remember that you
will not read the secondaries with the same definition value as you use for
the primaries. These are only indicators of second efforts, or second effort

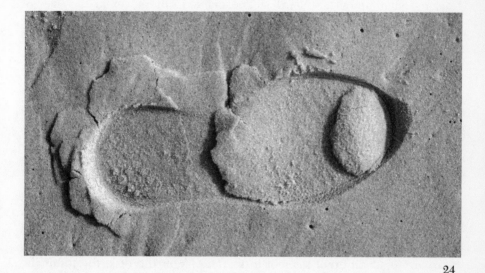

24

series, which depict how intense was the second effort. In the illustration you will see a primary dish-fissure; this tells you that the human is at a slow run. However, the first and strongest secondary is a dish, showing the first of the secondary efforts. This is followed by a disk-fissure, which shows the second secondary effort, then finally the disk, which shows the third and final secondary effort.

These secondaries show the battle between the intended speed and the outside forces. Generally any more than one or two secondaries is a wasted or inefficient effort. When I coach world-class runners, using the wisdom of the pressure releases, I try to get their running prints to contain one primary and just one secondary. By eliminating all others their energy is focused and better channeled into their run. They are faster and more efficient, less fatigued, and less prone to injury. However, variations in landscapes, even slight, can cause an excess of secondaries. These landscape variations will be easily recognized because of their landscape-imposed distortion nature.

Not long after you begin to work in the tracking box and in other tracking environments, you will notice marked differences in the sizes of disks and dishes. These differences are of tremendous significance and must be defined here so that there is no confusion. Just as in the last pressure release study, dealing with the pressure against the wall, the sizes are defined in eights and in proportion to the track. I will not accept from my students the term disk or dish alone, for they must be defined. Each eighth gradation of these pressure releases is extremely significant to the speed and forward motion of that human or animal. Thus we need to know how large a disk or dish is.

Illustration 31 shows a human footprint with the disk and dish dividing line. Looking at the forward portion of the foot you will notice a curved line, drawn to depict a disk that is one-eighth the distance between the toe and the dividing line. This then is called an eighth disk. Moving to the next line, we now have a quarter disk, followed by a three-eighths disk, followed by a half disk, to a five-eighths disk, and so on to a full disk. In other words there are eight different sizes of disks. The larger the disk, the faster the speed. So too, looking behind the dividing line you will find an eighth dish, followed by a quarter dish, and so on to a full dish. Again there are eight different sizes of dishes. The larger the dish, the faster the speed. Then, once the dish exceeds the heel we have a dish that is called a *washover*.

What is true of the disks and dishes is also true of the disk-fissures and disk-crumbles and with the dish-fissures and dish-crumbles. These too are divided into eights. So there are eight gradations of disks, eight gradations of disk-fissures, eight gradations of disk-crumbles, eight gradations of dishes, eight gradations of dish-fissures, eight gradations of dish-crumbles, the washover, the washover-fissure, and the washover-crumble. Given the original six disks and dishes, which have now expanded into forty-eight increments, adding the three new washovers, the wave, the double wave, and the explode-off, you now have fifty-four primary pressure releases dealing with forward motion. Add now the fifty-four secondaries (yes, they also are incremented), and you will have learned 108 pressure releases in this study.

What does all of this staggering expansion mean? It's actually quite simple. You can no longer say a "slow jog" is a "disk-fissure," for now you have eight gradations of a slow jog, which means eight different speeds that can still be considered a jog. What this gives you as a tracker is such a speed sensitivity that to duplicate this same sensitivity an automobile speedometer

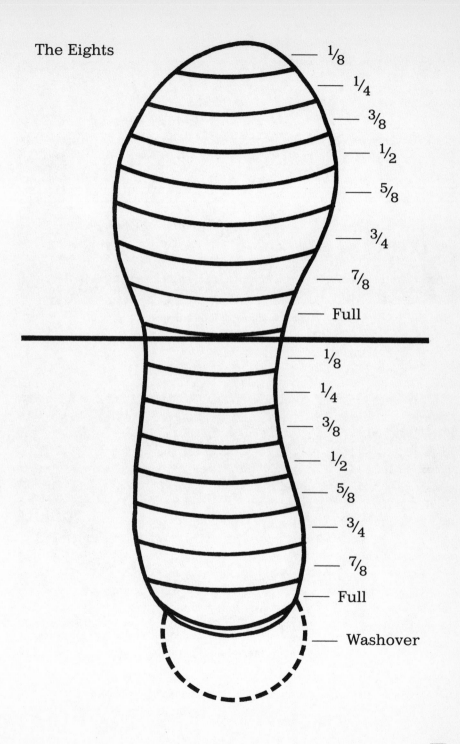

The Eights

— 1/8
— 1/4
— 3/8
— 1/2
— 5/8
— 3/4
— 7/8
— Full

— 1/8
— 1/4
— 3/8
— 1/2
— 5/8
— 3/4
— 7/8
— Full

— Washover

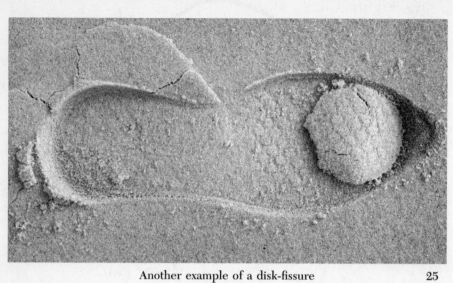

Another example of a disk-fissure   25

Another example of a dish-crumble   26

would have to stretch clear across the dashboard. With all animals, including the human animal, the same rule of the eights applies. Now you have eight gradations of a fast walk, a trot, a bound, a lope, and a gallop, as well as eight gradations in each increment of the human walk. Forward motion is much more complex than it seems.

By this point, we can tell if the animal or human has changed direction, slowed, or stopped. We also know exactly how fast that animal is going and how much second effort it is taking to maintain that speed. Now we will move into our third pressure release study, in which we will find out exactly how an animal is holding its head and in which direction it is looking. Slowly but surely we are beginning to look deep into an animal's actions, thoughts, and emotions.

8. ROLL AND HEAD POSITION

We have thus far discovered how to tell if an animal has changed direction and how to accurately determine its speed. In this present study, we will deal with how the animal is holding its head and in what direction he is looking, in any given track. Out of all of the pressure release studies, this is by far the easiest to learn. In fact it takes no time at all. Right after reading this, with no tracking box time, you can go out and put it to use with 100 percent accuracy. Actually, it is so simple that I am almost embarrassed to include it in this book. Yet having met so many other good trackers, I'm still surprised that not one of them seemed aware of this simple concept of determining head position.

Before we go any further I want you to do a little experiment. First of all, get down on your hands and knees, lifting the feet well off the ground so only your knees are touching. Now move your head back and forth, then up and down. What did you find? That's right, not only did your hands shift pressure with your head movements but so did your knees. In fact, the shift was so powerful in your knees that your feet actually moved from side to side, up and down with the action of your head. What does all this mean? Simply that whatever the front feet go through the rear feet must also go through when it comes to the positioning of the head. Knowing the reaction of your rear feet you can understand why, in this study, you do not need to worry whether the foot is a front foot or a rear foot. You can get the same information from any of the feet.

Let's begin this section with a discussion of what we call *roll*. This roll factor determines if the head is held high or low and every other level in between. Refer now to illustration 32a, b, and c. Here I have drawn these tracks in the same way I drew them in the last pressure release study. In other words, the track heel enters from the left, compresses the floor, then exits to the right. These pressure releases differ from how you have come to know them—these have little to do with building up anything, and everything to do with pressure and the depth of the track.

In illustration 32a you will note that the heel of the track and the toe of the track are of equal depth. This means that the animal's head is held in what is called the neutral position (depicted in the line drawing of the head and back of the animal above the track illustration). This is one of the more comfortable positions to hold the head—you will typically see animals walking with their heads in this position. I sometimes even call this the

95

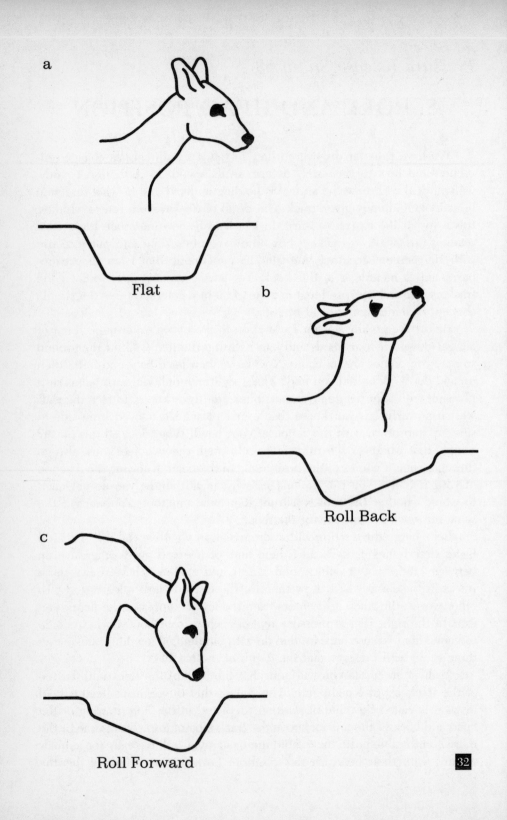

a

Flat

b

Roll Back

c

Roll Forward

32

neutral walking position. It means that the animal is at ease and generally only mildly alert.

In illustration 32b you will see that I have drawn the heel section of the track deeper than the toe section. This indicates that the animal's weight is back on the heels, which means its head is in an upright alert position, as depicted by the line drawing of the animal above.

Finally, looking at illustration 32c, you will note that I have drawn this track with the toe section much deeper than the heel. This means that the animal's weight is forward and down, thus the head is down in a sniffing or feeding position, also shown in the line drawing of the animal's head.

Though these tracks are drawn a bit more dramatically than they actually appear in reality, there is still a marked difference even under the most difficult tracking conditions. I drew the three basic positions—head high, neutral, and down—to make the roll pressure releases a little easier to understand. Actually there are eight head positions all together and these eight positions can only be learned through experience. Yet to be more definitive, there are eight primary positions and eight secondary positions. To learn all of them you need more than just the tracks, you need to watch animals, and watch them a lot, always comparing their movements to what you find in the tracks after they leave. By now I don't think you will find it surprising to learn that these head positions are also measured in eights and have both primaries and secondaries.

Now that you have a way of telling the exact roll position of the head—how high or low it is being held, relative to its range—you must go a step further. Now we will discuss how to tell exactly which way the animal is looking. These pressure releases are called simply *head position* and work independently of the roll. Again, this study has everything to do with pressure and depth of the track, and little to do with the building up of any pressure releases as in past studies. Refer now to illustrations 33 a, b, c, d, and e. In these tracks I have shaded the deepest part of the print, and left unshaded those parts that are of equal depth.

In track 33a you will note that the outside right toe is the deepest, while the other three toes are shallow. This means that the animal is looking to its right, in the direction of the arrow. Remember that the back feet—all feet—will show this same depth in looking to the right. Now in track 33b I have shaded the outside right toe again along with the toe next to it, which means that the animal is looking in the direction of this arrow. In track 33c I have shaded only the toe to the right of center and this indicates that the animal is looking in the direction of this arrow. In track 33d, I have shaded

Head Position

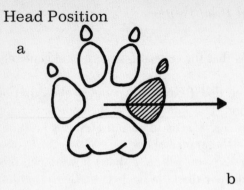

a

b

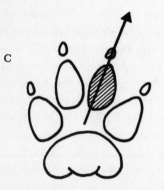

c

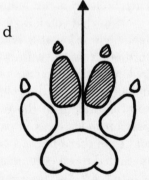

d

e

33

the center two toes, which then indicate the animal is looking straight ahead. Finally in track 33e I have shaded the right outside toe and the right outside heel. This indicates that the animal is looking over its shoulder and to the right.

Sound simple? Well, it is that simple. All you need now is a little experience. You might be wondering if a roll could interfere with head position. Absolutely not. If the animal's head was in a down position, all the toes would be of equal depth. But if the head was down while the animal was looking to the right, the outer right toe would be even deeper than all the rest of the toes. Of course the heel would show up shallower than the toes. Again, there are actually eight primary head positions and eight secondary head positions, just as in the roll pressure releases. Practice and experience will define them.

Actually I consider roll and head position pressure releases to be rather crude measurements. We will refine these measurements to precision in the next pressure release study. To me, roll and head position are defined in such increments that you can basically tell if the animal is looking toward 12:00, 1:00, 2:00, and so on. Add this basic knowledge to the refinement of the next pressure release study and you can tell exactly what the animal is looking at. In other words it becomes so precise you are able to say that the animal is looking at 1:18 and 16 seconds.

Another problem that will be cleared up in the next study is the confusion of *sweep*. Sweep is when the animal looks in several different directions before he goes on to the next track. After the next pressure release study, not only will you be able to see each of the increments he looked at during track placement, but you'll be able to tell exactly what he looked at and for how long. The next study will also further refine the change of direction to pinpoint accuracy. But before we go on to the next study, let's back up, clarify, and expand on a few things.

The first three major studies of pressure releases, which we've now covered, are in fact quite easy to master. As I stated earlier, many of my students find that they have a firm understanding of pressure release studies 1, 2, and 3 after an average of four hours in the tracking box. Most will agree that within ten hours of tracking box work they are well on their way to mastery. Remember that I deal with thousands of students every year and get constant feedback from them about their previous classes, and how far they have come. That is why I am so confident that you too will be able to do the same with a little time and effort in that tracking box.

The use of the tracking box, or at least an outside damp sandy area, is essential to understanding the pressure releases. To begin your study in difficult tracking areas will only create confusion. However, after that initial ten hours of study in the tracking box, you should begin to spend more time in other outside environments. Take it slow and easy as this natural transition takes place. Move from the box to an easy-tracking soil outside, like garden soil or a plowed field. Then move to the forest loams, then to more gravelly soil, then to the forest debris situations, and finally to the hard surfaces. All of these tracking areas, their personalities, and soil personalities will be discussed near the end of the book.

For the first forty hours of dirt time, you should concentrate exclusively on pressure release studies 1, 2, and 3. You need a firm foundation and understanding of these before you undertake studies 4, 5, and 6. These last three studies tend to be a bit more difficult and need a lot of experimentation on your part. To go on to these studies prematurely will only create confusion. So concentrate on, learn, and fully understand pressure release studies 1, 2, and 3 before moving ahead. Again, a good time indicator is that forty-hour mark. I would also suggest that you keep a tracking notebook, which not only records your progress but also the time you spend on each study.

MODIFYING YOUR TRACKING BOX

Now, after the initial forty to sixty hours of study in your tracking box, it is a good idea to modify the box in preparation for the next step. To do this, first remove all the sand and allow it to dry out. Cut another eight-foot board in half, and use the pieces to divide the box into three equal compartments. Reline each compartment with plastic and put the sand back into each. This gives you three separate compartments—and you can give each its own personality. This three-compartment box will become critical in your quest to understand soil personality and movement. It must be done if you are to advance your understanding and to learn fully the various formation quirks of the pressure releases.

In the first compartment, prepare the sand as you always did. Dampen it down, rake it, and smooth it with a board. This is the kind of zero earth you have been working with for the last forty to sixty hours, and this will be your starting point for the comparisons that must follow. In the second compartment, just dump in the dry sand and smooth it out. Do not dampen it in any way. In the last compartment, prepare the sand as you did in the first compartment, but instead of smoothing it down with a board, pound

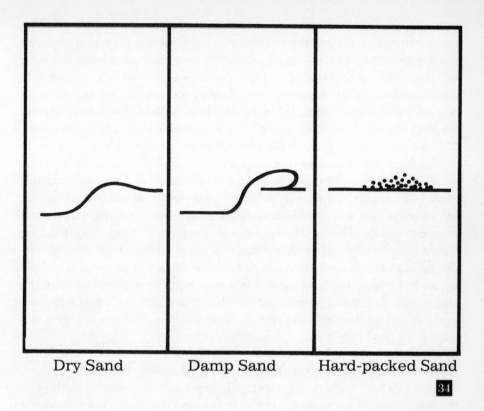

Dry Sand   Damp Sand   Hard-packed Sand

34

the sand with a heavy flat object, like a cement block, until it becomes rock hard. So hard, in fact, that you should hardly be able to press your thumb into it to create a track. The box is now ready for experimenting with soil personality.

To use this box, walk into the compartment with the normal damp sand, and make a turn. See illustration 34. You will see a plate form at the heel as you have seen it so many times before. Again, the pressure releases thrown in this box are those that you are most familiar with. Now repeat the same motion in the dry sand, and repeat the same motion again in the hard-packed sand. You will find that in the dry sand the same plate is more humped and rounded, thus depicting the pressure release personality of dry conditions. In the hard-packed sand, you will find that the plate is nothing more than a "pooling," or gathering, of sand grains, rather than the larger, more dramatic plate that you are familiar with.

What you have right before you is the same movement, the same pressure releases, but you also have the personality of each pressure release under different soil conditions. They are all still plates, they all depict that same movement, but they are all a little different. You must learn this basic soil personality difference of all pressure releases before you can begin to understand all the other, more complicated, soil personality and pressure release combinations. Yet, by beginning here in this three-compartment tracking box, you will find that all the rest is easier than it first appears. This box now becomes the basic foundation for all other soil studies.

I cannot stress enough the importance of dirt time, especially in the pressure release studies. Not just random dirt time, or haphazard practice time, but time spent following a logical progression of understanding. Far too many people want to learn something only from reading, rather than from experience. That is why we have so many people out there teaching things from theory rather than from experience. Don't rush through this dirt time; instead, take it slow and easy. Given the hectic personal schedules we all face today, the tracking box becomes even more valuable. With the box in your basement or just outside the house, coming home late from work should no longer be a concern. Your tracking medium is only a few steps away, and your tracking time starts immediately.

Eventually you will want to add variety to your tracking box experience. After a while, people walking through the box become all too easy to read. Then, if you have pets—dogs, cats, birds, or whatever—waltz them through the box. Watch them carefully as they move and then see what their tracks look like. Go into your box with bare feet; carrying a heavy object on your back, in your hand, in your arms; or after drinking a glass of water. Then see what the tracks tell you. Walk through the box when you are depressed, happy, hungry, thirsty, angry, or anything else. In other words, *practice and experiment.* The more you use the box, the more you experiment, the better tracker you are going to be.

9. DIGITAL PRESSURE RELEASES

Here is where the pressure release studies become a bit more complicated and demanding. Initially, I was just going to briefly define pressure
release studies 4, 5, and 6 for this book, but then I felt that this would leave
the reader with far too many questions. I know that it will not be long
before the reader, like all of my other students, will begin to see these more
advanced pressure releases and want to know why they are there and what
they mean. To avoid creating a huge blank space in people's understanding
of pressure releases, then, I have to treat pressure release studies 4, 5, and
6 more fully. Still, I am concerned about including them in this book for
fear of creating confusion due to what these studies demand of both student
and reader.

My greater apprehension, perhaps, is that the reader might not understand what I am presenting. Yet that fear only arises because I know that
without substantial practice and experimentation, no one could understand
these last three studies. So it is with this in mind that I am cautiously
proceeding. All that I can say is that you will, without a doubt, understand
these studies if you study religiously.

If you do not put in the practice time and the experimentation time,
then you will never understand these last three studies. The burden is now
on your shoulders.

Consider now that you can tell if an animal has changed direction,
slowed, or stopped, using the eleven primary and eleven secondary pressure
releases of the pressure against the wall study. You also know how fast an
animal is going, with the fifty-four primary and fifty-four secondary pressure
releases of the forward motion study. And you know how an animal is holding its head and in what direction it is looking. Given all the primaries and
secondaries of all the studies thus far, you have learned 130 distinct pressure
releases. That does not include the roll or head position pressure releases
of the last study. Now in a few short pages, you will not only double what
you know, but refine movements to pinpoint accuracy.

It is important to look at tracks in a different way now. Instead of
viewing the track as a whole, as we did in the first three pressure release
studies, we now divide it into sections of track anatomy. In essence, a track
is the end result of many track parts coming together to make the whole.
Each part, or section, of the track, though connected to the whole in the
final analysis, can and will work independently of the whole. It is this in-

dependent track part function that we will be looking into next, discovering how each of these parts works and how each creates and influences the whole.

That may sound complicated, but it really isn't. These independent track parts are the digits (toes), the heel pad, the lobes, and the toe ridges. Simply put, we set aside the entire track view and concentrate now on each of the parts. Each part produces its own movements and its own pressure releases, and has its own personality. Bringing all the parts together at the end will produce the final track. With this in mind, and going in the opposite direction, we can read the track to define major movements, but then we must move to the individual track parts to read the smaller movements and functions. Here in this study we will be isolating the digits; thus this study is called the digital pressure releases.

Again, reading the overall track, the entire track, allows us to see the major movements of the human or animal. To get to the deeper, more refined movements we must break the track down into its individual parts. For it is here in the individual parts that the tiniest movements are recorded, which in the end come together to form the whole. The easiest way to view these parts, such as the digits, is as if each digit were in fact a track in and of itself. Now consider the possibilities of these tracks within tracks. I said that these were definitely related to, yet semi-independent of, the whole. If you can begin to understand now what I am talking about, then the next statement will not take you by surprise.

Viewing each track part as a track in and of itself, we find that we have several tracks that, as a group, make up the digits. Each digit then is a track. Remember back when I said that all earth moves the same way? Well, couple this statement with the fact that each digit is a separate track and you will have doubled all the pressure releases that you know. Yes, that's right! All the 22 pressure releases for pressure against the wall, and the 108 pressure releases for forward motion are found again, though in miniature, inside each of the digits. The only thing you have to do is to put the qualifying word *digital* in front of them. For instance: a digital disk-fissure with a secondary digital disk. Notice that the word *digital* is used to define the pressure release. If you left out the word *digital*, I would assume you were talking about the first three pressure release studies.

Yes, you now have digital cliffs, ridges, peaks, crests, crest-crumbles, caves, cave-ins, plate-fissures, plate-crumbles, and explosions. You also have not only the digital primaries but also the digital secondaries. You have digital waves, double waves, disks, disk-fissures, disk-crumbles, dishes, dish-

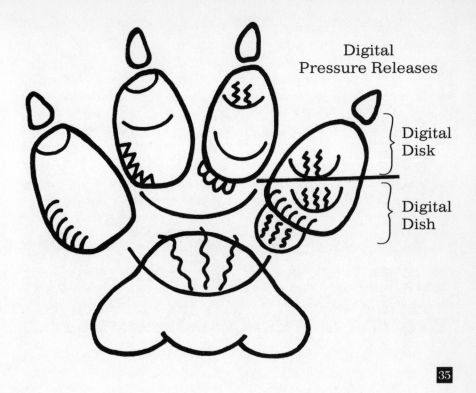

Digital
Pressure Releases

Digital
Disk

Digital
Dish

35

fissures, dish-crumbles, and explode-offs. With these, too, you have digital primaries and secondaries, as well as all the eights. Quite staggering, to say the least, but not overwhelming. It really is all so simple. You may be wondering where the dividing line between a digital disk and a digital dish is located. Simply cut the toeprint in half with a line so that both halves are of equal measurement. Anything forward of the line is a digital disk and anything behind it is a digital dish.

If you can understand that the toe print, the digit, is like an individual track and all earth moves the same way, then you can also understand how each of the digits can have its own separate pressure releases. Your biggest question right now should be how to know that a pressure release is a digital and not a major pressure release as defined in the first three studies. To give you a simple answer: basically it lies in the size and location of the pressure release. See illustration 35 and photo 27. You will note here that I have drawn into the digit several pressure releases. All of these are digital because of where they are found and how big they are.

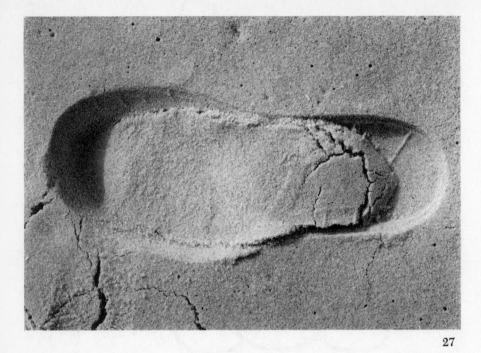

27

I know that location of these digital pressure releases is easy to understand but the size factor seems to be subject to interpretation. It may seem
that way at first, but there are other factors involved with determining size
and even location. Simply ask yourself these questions when trying to determine the size of the pressure release (which, in turn, will define the
pressure release as digital or not): What made this pressure release and how
was it made? Was it made by the entire track, through the joint effort of
several track parts, or by only one part, or digit, in particular? Now, let's
go on to clarify these questions further.

If the entire track comes together to create the pressure release then
there will be evidence in each part of the track pointing to the end result
(see illustration 36a, b, and c). In other words, all of the track parts will be
working together in harmony to complete one smooth movement or action.
In illustration 36a, I have drawn a plate-fissure off the side of the heel. You
will note that all the toes are sweeping together and shifting to the right at
the same time, where the toes pivot as one to produce the overall movement. These combined efforts of all track parts work together as a whole

a
Entire Track
Harmony

b
Partial
Harmony

c
Individual
Digit

to produce those larger pressure releases you have learned in the first three studies.

Looking now at illustration 36b, you will note that several of the digits have worked together to produce a major pressure release. Even though the combined efforts of just three digits produced this pressure release it is not considered a digital pressure release. It is too large and it was not made by only one digit.

Finally, in illustration 36c, you will see a true digital pressure release. This is quite easy to spot because this pressure release was made independently of all the other digits, and, for that matter, independently of everything else. You will note that the other digits have no corresponding movements or pressure releases that have anything to do with making the digital pressure release drawn. In fact, they appear to be totally detached from the digit creating the pressure release.

It is a pressure release's origin that defines it as being digital or some other pressure altogether. All you have to do is to isolate the particular digital pressure release, then make sure that the other digits did not have any assistance in the creation of that particular pressure release. However, though the digit will operate independently, the other digits, and other parts of the track, will show movements supporting that digital pressure release. Supporting pressure releases do not mean that they assisted that digit in the creation of its own pressure release. It only indicates other motions that correspond to the digital pressure release you are studying.

A good example of assistance digital pressure releases can be found in illustration 37. As you can see, the outside right digit in this drawing has thrown a small plate and on the inside there is a disk. Yet none of the other digits have this plate and disk. If any of the other digits had shown any sign of wall pressure in the same location then it would no longer be a digital pressure release. However, on the inside right digit there is an upper, inside crest-crumble. Together they depict a state of indecision. If either of these digital pressure releases was missing then it would not mean a state of indecision at all, but something entirely different. Yet it would still remain a digital pressure release in the outermost right digit.

Here's one other point about the assistance of other digits in creating a pressure release, and how to tell if that pressure release is made by the entire track, a portion of that track, or an individual part, in this case a digit. *Stiffness* is another factor that tells you that the pressure release is not from the digit. The movement of all the digits together creates a quite rigid effect. On the other hand, there is a lack of stiffness when individual digital pres-

Assistance Pressure Releases

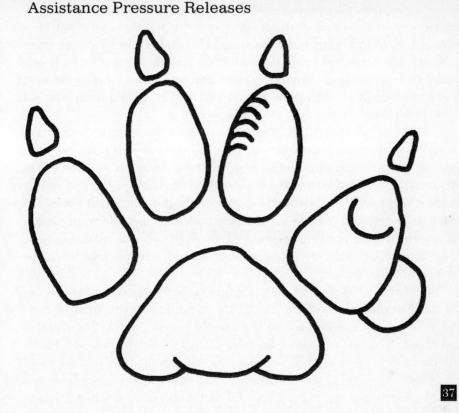

37

sure releases are thrown. This lack of stiffness can especially be felt in the big toe of a human. While standing on the broad part of a length of two-by-four board in bare feet, close your eyes. Immediately you will find your balance impaired and you will begin to wobble a bit. During this loss of balance pay rapt attention to your feet. You will find that your big toe seems to work independently of every other part of your foot. In fact you will find many parts of your foot working independently of each other. And sometimes they will work together—at those times you will notice an overall stiffness.

This is exactly what happens with individual digital pressure releases. The digits work in much the same way as did your big toe in the last exercise. And at other times, just as you felt in your foot, all components of that foot work together. You may now be concerned about the possibility—a high probability at that—of there being a combination of several major motions where all parts of the foot work together, followed by a combination of individual digital motions. This does occur in almost every track and what you have to do is read all of it in the correct order it was made. Part of this concern will be taken care of as we get into the next illustrations, and the rest will be taken care of when we get to the section called "Individual Track Analysis" in chapter 12.

As I previously stated, digital pressure releases define not only direction change with precision, but also head position and roll with pinpoint accuracy. Of course, many more intricate areas and movements involved are in the digital pressure releases, and these will be discussed at the end of this chapter. Right now let's look at illustration 38. In this illustration I combine some major pressure releases for changing and maintaining forward motion with several digital pressure releases. This will give you an indication as to how these digital pressure releases function and subsequently how they interact with each other.

In illustration 38 you will note that there is a primary dish-fissure in the heel, followed by a secondary disk in the toe ridge area in front of that. This tells you the speed of the animal and the secondary effort to maintain that speed. Now you will notice an array of digital pressure releases. In the outermost right digit you will notice a two-quarters digital dish-fissure and a half secondary digital disk-fissure. It is important to note again here that these changing and maintaining forward motion pressure releases found in the digits do not necessarily have to do with its forward motion, though most of the time forward motion is the case. You will also note that there is a digital plate-fissure in the lower inside of the digit with a secondary digital crest.

In the inner right digit you will find a half digital dish and a half secondary digital disk. You will also find that the inside center of this digit has a small plate. Moving on, you will discover that I have drawn, in the inner left digit, a quarter digital dish and an eighth secondary digital disk-fissure. Also you will note that there is a digital crest on the lower outside of the digit. Finally, the left digit has an eighth digital disk and on the lower outside, a small ridge. Combined, all of these digital pressure releases tell a story, contributing to the major motion, yet independent of each other in movement. What you are looking at is a drawing copied from a real track, and this is the kind of combination of pressure releases you will find in all tracks.

Digital Pressure
Release Analysis

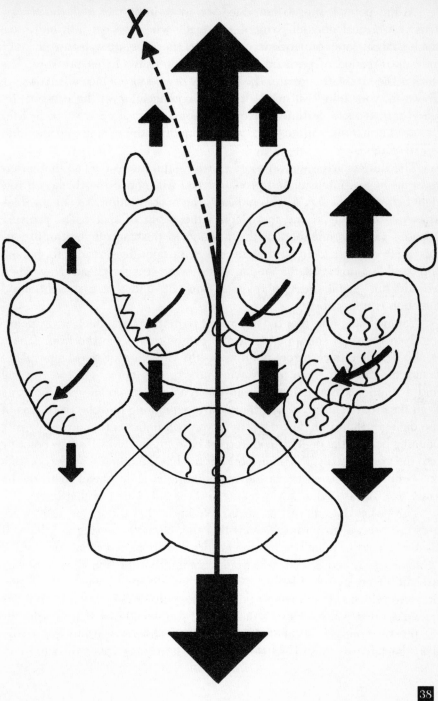

At this point I want to introduce you to an important tool: the arrows. This is a critical notation symbol, especially when we get into individual track analysis later on. Arrows drawn into the pressure releases not only indicate direction of pressure but also the intensity of that pressure. The thicker the arrow, the greater the intensity of pressure. Once all arrows are drawn in, your mind will move from the complication of the pressure releases into the simpler linear arrow notations. Magically a flow, or feel for the track's motion, will develop, which simplifies the overall and the individual analyses.

The thicker arrows mean more pressure and intensity. The thinner arrows mean less intensity and pressure. You will notice the thickest arrow right behind the heel pad. This indicates the major motion. An equally thick arrow at the front of the foot depicts the result of that major pressure release—i.e., forward motion, the reaction to pushing off. Up until now, this is all you've had to work with and, with only this broad information, you would assume that the animal was moving straight ahead. Now when we add the digital pressure releases, you will find that a straight-ahead direction is impossible.

You will note now that the outermost right digit has a thick arrow pointing from the rear, and an equal arrow pointing out from the front. There is also a rather thick arrow pointing in the direction of the digital plate-fissure area of that same toe. Moving now to the inner right toe you will find a thinner arrow pointing from the rear and its counterpart pointing from the front. There's also a thinner arrow pointing into the plate area of the digit. In the inside left digit, now, you will notice a thinner arrow still, pointing behind the digit, its counterpart in front, and a small arrow pointing into the crest. Finally, the innermost left toe has the thinnest arrow pointing out behind with a reactionary arrow pointing straight ahead, both of the same size. Another thin arrow points into the ridge area of that digit.

Now what does all of this mean? We know that the major dish-fissure pressure release in the heel means that the animal is moving at a lope. If all you had at this point was just the major pressure releases that you learned in studies 1, 2, and 3, then you would assume that the animal was moving straight ahead, as I said before. Now let's unleash the magic of the digital pressure releases. If you were to draw a line cutting the track bilaterally, as shown, so that you have two equal halves, you would find that, judging by the pressure releases of the digits, the right two toes are pushing off harder than the left two toes. Thus the right side is moving faster than the left.

The analysis then dictates that the animal is not moving straight ahead, as originally thought, but turning slightly to the left.

To show you what I mean I'll use a rather large example. Let's say you are driving a bulldozer and you want to turn to the left. You have two options. You can either speed up the right track or slow down the left. In other words, the right side must push off harder and cover more distance than the left, to make you turn left. Basically this is what is happening to the track in our illustration. The left side is a little slower and the right side a little faster. With the use of these pressure releases you can easily see a forward motion change in direction that would not have been discernible in pressure release studies 1, 2, or 3. But it is a change of intense precision. It is like saying that the animal turned from 12:00 to 12:00 and 30 seconds, referring back to the example of turning we used in the first pressure release study.

One of the more frequently asked questions whenever I use this illustration is: What if the animal is actually turning to the right, dragging his right two toes backward and subsequently throwing the digital forward motion pressure releases? Well, that would be impossible given the *pivot factor*. Notice the pressure against the wall and the arrows. This pressure against the wall was caused by the pivoting of the toes into the left walls of the tracks. If the animal had indeed turned to the right then the pressure against the wall would be to the right side of each toe. Usually no pressure release can stand alone. Instead it is a series of checks and balances, justifications, correlations, and other defining and proving factors.

It is poor practice to isolate just one part of the track and try to glean a true meaning from that reading. Instead you should scrutinize each part, bring all corresponding parts together, then move to the overall picture. Every individual part of the track has to agree with each other and then be justified with the whole. In fact, even the slightest movement can be justified or proved against every other track in that track series. *Track series* is defined as all the tracks that were in contact with the ground when the motion was made. If you are reading intricate digital pressure releases in the right front track, then the left rear will also show evidence of your findings. After all, the animal or human being tracked is a single harmonious entity. Can an animal change direction, be hungry, pregnant, or anything else only in a certain select foot? Absolutely not.

But what about humans and, even more challenging, what about humans with their shoes on? It's obvious that humans in bare feet do have digital pressure releases. After all, the barefoot human track has obvious toe prints. The same rule applies to the digital pressure releases of humans as to those of their animal brothers and sisters. But surely shoes, you may be saying, pose another problem. You may think that it is impossible to see anything this subtle in their tracks. After all, you're trying to read digital pressure releases through thick rubber or leather. Well, they can be seen right through the deadening effects of modern footwear. True, at first they are invisible to you, but through practice and experimentation you will soon see them. The only quirk is that they are "muffled," but they are very discernible. Yeah, you have to pay your dues—the dues of dirt time.

I am now at the point of most concern. A concern that will follow me through the next two pressure release studies. It would be virtually impossible to cover in a book every conceivable bit of information that the digital pressure releases convey to you. It would take volumes, at the very least. Even then, I really do not think that I could put all of it into words. What I am going to discuss next holds true, not only for this pressure release study, but for the pressure release studies that follow. At this point, and only with this study, the one thing you have in your favor is that 90 percent of the digital study deals with precision direction change. The other 10 percent deals with a multitude of topics, from slowing, to head position, to balance compensation, and many more.

So how do you learn the 10 percent left out of this study, and all of the information yet to come, that cannot be fully explained in a book? To put it succinctly: *experiment*. What do I mean? You have to develop now the same passion—nearly obsession—that I had as a child and that has followed me throughout my life. Grandfather expected practice, for he had the same problem I do with teaching this. But as far as Grandfather was concerned, he expected intense practice, experimentation, and passion for knowledge. He would not hand me anything. In fact, he never laid out the pressure releases as I have for you. He would simply point to a pressure release and ask, "What dis mean?" I not only had to figure out what the pressure release meant out of context but eventually had to place it in some order. You have it all.

So what do I mean by experimentation with a passion? First I would use my own body as an experimentation medium. I would come home starving and walk through the tracking box, then eat a big meal and walk through the tracking box and isolate the differences. If nature called and I had to go to the bathroom, before hitting the toilet I would hit the tracking box, then hit it again after I relieved myself. I did this when I had an injury, a cold, a headache, when I was thirsty, and in countless other conditions. I would hit the tracking box when I was angry, infuriated, apprehensive, depressed, happy, joyous, and every other emotion I could isolate.

I then graduated to experimenting with animals. First the family dog. I would waltz him through the tracking box just before I fed him, then allow him to eat, periodically pulling him away from his dinner to check his tracks as his belly got slowly full. I would do the same thing before I walked him and after I got back. Always laying the tracks down side by side to each other, like a before and after analysis right in the same place. I would invite friends over, I would invite my friends' pets over, anything to get a variety and subsequently find a similarity in what I was reading in the tracks.

I then moved afield. I would watch a deer defecate then go over to read the pressure releases before the pile of scat and after. I would watch a fox kill a rabbit then observe the tracks before and after. I would watch an animal walking at peace in the forest, purposely make a slight sound to alert him, then compare the tracks from before the sound was heard and after the sound was heard. The possibilities were endless. It was never a chore, for my passion and obsession for answers would never allow it to become a chore or boring. Just finding the differences in track extremes for me was never enough. I also had to know every increment of change in between. For instance, the stomach of an animal being full or empty was but a small part of the story. I needed to know how much food was actually in the animal's belly, exactly how thirsty he was, how aware or frightened, and so on. I demanded nothing less than total knowledge.

I also was not satisfied doing a comparative analysis only once or with just one species. Once was not enough, a thousand times were not enough; there was never enough, no matter how many times I did a comparative analysis. The question to you is this: How badly do you want to understand all of this? If only mildly, then stick with pressure release studies 1, 2, and 3, for those take very little time. But if you want it more than anything else, then you have the passion—make the time, and you will master this study and the two others that follow. I, personally, am never satisfied with superficial knowledge. I want it all, even to this day. The fires of passion have never died in me. I am always tracking, always experimenting, always pushing the limits.

10. LOBULAR PRESSURE RELEASES

At this point you have learned in the first two pressure release studies 130 pressure releases, and another 8 pressure releases from pressure release study 3. From these pressure releases you can tell the direction changes of an animal or human, slowing and stopping, and major shifts in the body weight. You also can define the exact speed of that human or animal with incredible accuracy, as well as define the secondary efforts needed to maintain that speed. You can also tell exactly the way the head is being held and in what direction the animal or human was looking when he or she made the track.

Added to that knowledge are the 130 digital pressure releases, bringing your total up to 268 defined pressure releases. The first three pressure release studies dealt with major motions; the digital pressure releases and the studies beyond begin to refine and define precisely those major motions. In other words, with pressure release studies 4, 5, and 6, we are not only moving into the inner workings of the animal's body, but eventually into its mind and emotional state. With each step, from the digitals, to the lobulars, and finally to the toe ridges, we learn to read the finer precision pressure release information.

Reviewing and expanding the information on the digital pressure releases at this point is critical, for it sets the groundwork for the next study. I have stressed heavily the need for dirt time, and especially for impassioned experimentation, in learning all of this. Earlier I said that most of my students gain a full understanding of pressure release studies 1, 2, and 3 in as little as four hours of dirt time. Within ten hours they are well on their way to mastery of these first three pressure release studies. Most of my graduates have told me that after the initial ten hours in the tracking box with the first three studies, most of them obtain a thorough understanding of the digital pressure releases with an additional forty hours' worth of dirt time. Forty hours of dirt time is not a lot of time if you are serious about learning how to track.

Certainly the major function of the digital pressure releases is to refine the exact change of direction of an animal. Also to determine precisely how the head is being held and where it is looking, and even what it may be looking at. Yet there is more. I did not want to get into the "more" until this point, the point at which you have accumulated some valuable dirt time. The digitals also indicate tail wag or sweep, coughing, sneezing, sniffing, major injuries and afflictions, later stages of pregnancy, extremes in body function like vomiting, constipation, overloaded bowel, and much more. Of course, the only way you can really learn these is by experimentation and dirt time.

As you see, the digital pressure releases tell you much more than precision direction changes and head positions. No sooner do you get into your experimentation than you begin to see these other indicators come to life through these same digital pressure releases. Yet the digitals are only the beginning. To me the digitals are like a transition from the major motions of the body into the more intimate arena of internal and external movements and functions. In this next study, the lobular pressure releases, we go to the very core of an animal's existence, probing deeper and deeper into the world of the animal. Deeper than you ever dreamed possible.

The lobular pressure releases do show deep inside the animal, right to the animal's or human's everyday body functions. It is through the lobulars that we can read the condition of the stomach—how full it is—as well as the condition of the small intestine, the large intestine, the bladder, and the colon. We can see the rhythm of the breathing, whether the animal is taking a breath in or out in any given track. We can read mild afflictions, such as a common cold, a slight injury, arthritic conditions, congestion, sniffling, as well as growling, grunting, and other vocal callings. Here too we can read countless other normal body functions, conditions, and internal movements. Yet here in the lobulars we are also connected to the finest outer body movements. Movements that cannot be picked up by the human eye, even as it physically watches that animal or human.

Soft external movements, they are called. Shivering, panting, degree of ear cocking, tongue position, hesitations, twitches, minute balance compensations, snarling, nose twitching, slight tail movements, and so many others are the soft external movements. But to identify, and understand, these deep internal and soft external movements, there is a price to pay. A price that is measured in countless hours of dirt time and intense, impassioned, almost obsessive experimentation. Here there is no magic number of hours needed for mastery. It is a constant growth that will stay with you for the rest of your life. It is a never-ending quest to read deeper and deeper into these pressure releases. I don't think that anyone can really exhaust all of the possibilities in one lifetime.

Here, as we begin to enter the lobular pressure releases study, I am faced with a tremendous dilemma. It is probably one of the two shortest chapters in this book, yet it is the one chapter that will take a lifetime to understand. I can only hope here that you can just understand the basics, and then surrender yourself to the fact that the only way you are going to learn these lobulars, and what they indicate, is through a lifetime of dirt time. My concern here is not that you may not understand the lobular concept, but that I cannot give you much more than you find here in this chapter. It would take far more space than this book could provide, than ten books could provide, and weeks of personal fieldwork under my direction, to begin to master these concepts.

Here and in the next pressure release study, all I can do is lay down the foundation, the concepts, and the rest will be up to you. Here is where the difficulty begins. More than in any other study, this will take intense observation and obsessive experimentation on your part. There is just no other way around it, but I will do all I can here in this chapter to make it as easy as possible for you. You must do exactly as I had to do under the tutelage of Grandfather. As I indicated before, he handed me nothing, and expected everything. Only you can make yourself a master tracker, only you can put in the dirt time.

We will begin by locating the lobular pressure releases, then move on to what they look like. Lobular pressure releases are found in the heel of the track, to the rear (see illustration 39). An animal may have one, two, three, four, or five lobes behind the heel, depending on its species. In some rare cases I have seen six and seven lobular positions, though these were an abnormality. Typically lobes come in ones, twos, and threes, with twos and threes being the most common. Humans also have lobes. Human lobes are located to the rear of the ball of the foot, and the pressure releases there follow the same set of rules as do the pressure releases for animals.

Lobulars also have two zones or regions. Refer now to illustration 40. You will see that a line has been drawn across the heel pad so that it just touches the confluence or junction of the lobes. The lobular regions are defined as having two equal hemispheres. The lower region runs from the line to the farthest point at the back of the heel pad. This distance is also used to define the upper region, which runs not from the line to the front of the heel pad, but from the line forward the exact same distance as the lower region. So the upper and lower regions of the lobes are equal in length. Note the dotted line marking the forward-most measurement of the upper lobe. The brackets define the two zones and the two equal measurements of those zones, or regions.

We now must look upon these lobes in the same way we did the digits of the last study. We must understand that each lobe is a track part, or

Location of
Lobulars

Lobular
Division

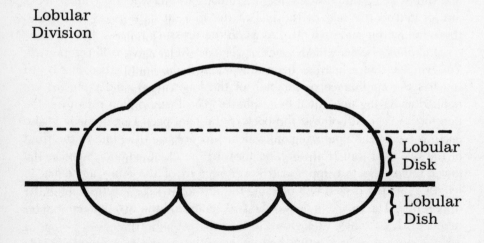

} Lobular
Disk

} Lobular
Dish

Lobular Pressure Releases

41

section, part of the whole, but with an ability to move independently. Thus we must view each lobe as a miniature separate track, just as we did for the digits. With this in mind, knowing that all earth moves in the same way and that each lobe is a track, then we also know that every pressure release found in the digits and found in the first three pressure release studies are now found in the lobes. Yes, double again all the pressure releases you know. Here, as in the last study, you must define the pressure release with the qualifier *lobular*. For instance: a lobular disk-fissure.

So we have lobular pressure against the wall, just as we had digital pressure against the wall. We have lobular cliffs, lobular ridges, lobular peaks, lobular crests, lobular crest-crumbles, lobular caves, lobular cave-ins, lobular plates, lobular plate-fissures, lobular plate-crumbles, lobular explosions, and all the lobular secondaries that go with them. We also have lobular waves, double waves, disks, disk-fissures, disk-crumbles, dishes, dish-fissures, dish-crumbles, and explode-offs. Again we have the lobular secondaries and all of the eight measurements, just as we did in the digital pressure releases. Only these lobulars are typically much smaller than the digital pressure releases.

The dividing line between the area of lobular disks and that of lobular dishes is that thick dividing line as seen in illustration 40. Simply, lobular disks fall in the upper region and lobular dishes fall in the lower region, or zone. Now refer to illustration 41. You will see that I have drawn a wide assortment of lobular pressure releases, both primary and secondary. In the outermost right lobe you will see a three-quarter lobular dish-fissure with a lobular secondary half disk-fissure. Also, coming off the inside of the lobe is a lobular plate with a secondary lobular crest.

Moving to the center lobe you will see that I have drawn a half lobular dish and a secondary quarter lobular disk. Here too on the center lobe you will find a small ridge. In the lobe to the left I have drawn a quarter lobular dish and a secondary eighth lobular disk-fissure. You now have 22 more lobular pressure releases against the wall and 108 lobular forward motion pressure releases. That includes all the primaries, secondaries, and eighths measurements. However, it must be noted here that the lobular forward motion pressure releases rarely have anything to do with forward motion. Yes, the lobe must move in the same way to produce them, but it is caused from a motion or function of the body and not forward motion.

What does all this mean? That is the problem. It can mean several different things, depending on what the pressure releases are like in the digital area. I figure that to cover every possible lobular pressure release combination would probably fill the better part of an encyclopedia. Even then, three-quarters could not be adequately explained or diagrammed. As I stated earlier, these lobular pressure releases deal with internal movements and functions, as well as small external motions. There is no way around the fact that you have to *experiment and practice*. This is the crux of my concern and why I struggled with the idea of not including it in this book.

However, at least I shall give you a bold example of how these lobular pressure releases work. Refer now to illustrations 42a, b, and c, where I have drawn three right rear tracks on the same page for easy comparison. In the center of the black box you will note that I have isolated the innermost lobe (illustration 42a). Notice here that I have also drawn in a one-eighth lobular disk in the front section of the lobe. I purposely left out the smaller (supporting backup and corresponding) pressure releases to minimize confusion. The location of this lobular disk and its size means that the animal's stomach is only one-eighth full. Please keep in mind, again, that I have left out several smaller pressure releases that would justify this statement.

Moving now to illustration 42b, you will see that there I have drawn a half lobular disk. This means that the animal's stomach has become half full. Finally, in illustration 42c, I have drawn in a seven-eighths lobular disk, which means that the animal's stomach is nearly full. Of course, and again, no pressure release can stand alone. In this case I left out the justification and corresponding pressure releases to minimize confusion. Out of the

Filling Stomach

a ⅛ Full

b ½ Full

c Full

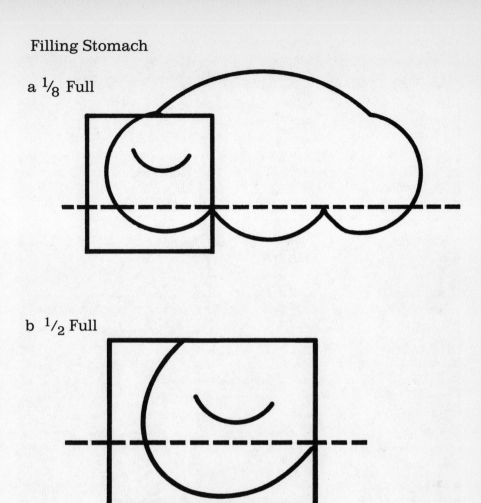
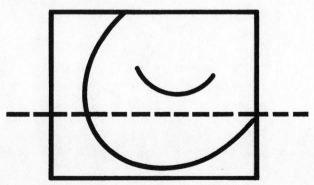

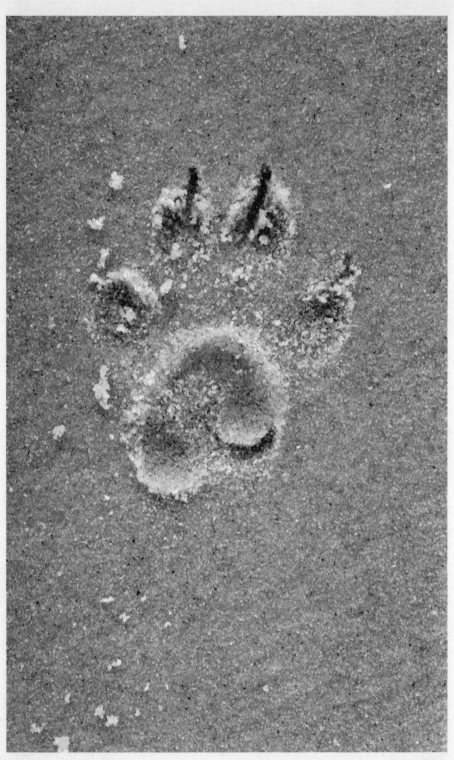

whole "stomach condition" lobular pressure release map, I chose the disks, for they are the largest, most obvious pressure releases that indicate the condition of the stomach.

Again you may be concerned that you might mix up a lobular pressure release with some of their larger cousins. The same rule of isolating and identifying that we used in locating the digital pressure releases applies to the lobular areas also. In other words, the lobes can stiffly become part of the overall track picture, thus the major pressure releases will be thrown. They can work together with other lobes, and still the pressure releases thrown will not be lobular. Only when they work alone can they throw a lobular pressure release. What you find in one particular lobe will have no bearing on what you find in all the others. Yet, in the final analysis, the lobular pressure releases are very small—extremely small—and located in or around the lobe area. Size and location are usually a dead giveaway.

Practice. Experiment. Begin with extremes so that there is no mistaking the pressure releases or what is happening to the track on the lobular level. I have already given several good examples of what you can try, like walking a dog through the box when he is very hungry and again when he has engorged himself. Then, after becoming familiar with the differences, begin to break it down by interrupting his dinner and walking him through the box. This way you get a progression of ever-increasing stomach content laid out side by side in your tracking box. Again, and again, all I can tell you is to practice and experiment with a passion bordering on obsession.

11. TOE RIDGE PRESSURE RELEASES

I have been hammering home the necessity of practice and experimentation for many chapters now, and I just can't stress it enough. Especially if you intend to learn and master pressure release studies 4, 5, and 6. When I ask people to experiment, they usually conjure up images of difficult tracking situations, taking pets into their tracking boxes, and watching, to the exclusion of everything else, the animals in general. This approach certainly is paramount, but start with a more familiar subject at first. Instead, you have all you need, right now, without any hassles. You have your tracking box and yourself. Who knows better what you are feeling than you? So "know thyself" first. You have digits, you have lobes, and you have toe ridges, just like all the other animals. Don't bite off more than you can chew by beginning your practice on animals.

First know everything about your own tracks, how they show what you are feeling and thinking, and even your internal condition. Once you master your own body recorded in your tracks, the transition to every other animal will be smooth and relatively easy. An intermediate step would be to study friends. They can also convey to you what they are experiencing and then you can prove it by their tracks. Let's face it, it's very hard to get a deer or fox to tell you that he is hungry and his bladder is full!

Now what do the toe ridge pressure releases convey to you? In the last pressure release study of lobulars, you learned that these pressure releases depict "soft" external movement as well as internal movement and conditions. The toe ridge pressure releases go one step beyond. Here, in the toe ridges, you will be able to read the finest internal movements, such as a swallow, a grimace, a moving gas bubble in the intestine, and much more. Now you will be able to read emotions and even thoughts, for this is where these deep processes record themselves, in the toe ridge pressure releases.

You are probably wondering how this could ever be recorded in any track. After all, emotions and thoughts do not have substance, weight, or form. I would only half agree with you, in that they do not have substance and weight, granted, but they certainly have form. What form? The form, or posture, your body assumes anytime you are wrapped in an emotion. Try this little experiment. First walk through your tracking box normally. Then sit down and think depressing or, conversely, joyous thoughts. Once overtaken by the emotion of either depression or joy, walk through the box again. You will definitely notice the difference. The tracks scream at you, for your whole body posture has changed dramatically.

Each emotion generates its own body posture. You must remember that the mind is a very powerful tool. The mind can turn any situation into a heaven or a living hell. These emotions, and many of the thought processes, imprint themselves on the body and subsequently to the tracks in virtually the same way. There are only so many emotions that we have to deal with, and understanding your body's reactions will make it easier to find similarities in other people and even animals. The precise body postures that originate in the emotions and thoughts are called physical emotion and physical thought personality, or identity.

Emotional identity is quite easy for most people, both experienced tracker and novice alike, to understand. For example, all of us have at one time experienced the body's emotional identity of depression. We walk with slumped shoulders, bowed head, dragging feet, lack of energy and drive, and fail to notice all that is around us. When we are joyous, even excited, our heads are held high, our shoulders back and square, and there is a definite bounce in our step. The personality of fear is one of confusion, nervousness, and apprehension, magnified through the body and into the feet, which show those traits. So too with anger, for the body becomes rigid, the feet pound the ground, and we walk with violence. More violent still is the physical personality of rage. These are just a few of the physical personalities of emotion that we have all experienced and can easily identify with. If we fail to notice these physical changes emotion causes in our own bodies, then we are simply out of touch with our bodies.

More difficult to discern than the physical personalities of emotion are the physical personalities of thought. Again I call upon you to use your own body and your own thoughts to experiment with; see how a thought shifts to the body, which, in turn, registers in the feet. A simple way to learn the physical manifestations of thought is to pay attention to what you are thinking and what effect it is having on your body.

For a dramatic example of the physical personality induced and directed by thought, let's say you are walking loosely in a straight line and suddenly something catches your eye to the right. You look, but you decide to continue on in the original route. Suddenly you get an urge to go back, and subsequently you think of making a hard right turn. Beyond the hesitation pressure releases, which can be found at a digital level, you will also see a reverberation pressure release, coupled with a slight sway to the right and a shift in strike dominance to the right foot. Strike dominance means the force at which your foot hits the ground. This body English—personality—born of thought will continue until you eventually make up your mind to turn or continue on.

Here again, the best way to learn this is to use first your own body and thoughts. While walking through the tracking box, think hard about making a right or left turn, speeding up, or slowing down (but just one thought). Now go back and read these pressure releases as compared to a straight-forward walk. The dramatic difference will appear in the resultant toe ridges found in your tracks. Try this with thought after thought, all the while paying attention to your body and the tracks being made. However, in all of these practice sessions using yourself for an example, it is best to use the real emotions or thoughts during the process. If you are depressed when you come home from work then hit the tracking box while you are still wrapped in this depression. To try to mimic or role-play these emotions is to get marginal and confusing results.

It is in the toe ridge that all emotion and thought are recorded. This toe ridge is influenced much like the pressure against the wall study, though in a subtle, miniature way. But where are the toe ridges found, how do toe ridge pressure releases work, and how are they formed? Refer now to illustration 43. You will notice that I highlighted the toe ridge area with a dark shading. Toe ridges are the "negative" part of the track, while the toes and heel pad are the "positive" part of the track. It is easy to understand where the toe ridges are located on a typical animal and human print, but you may be wondering where it is located in a deer print. The toe ridge on a deer print is the rise between the two parts of the hoof.

As you can clearly see from the illustration, not only do the toe ridges wrap around and lie between the toes, but they are also found between the toes and the heel pad. Because these toe ridges encompass each individual part of the track—they wrap nearly around each part, and are in contact with nearly every part at center track—they are like a link, a connection between all parts of the track. And, because they build so high and fragile, they are affected by even the slightest movement, function, or pressure change. They are one of the most sensitive areas of the track. The only place that you will find more sensitivity is with the macro and micro pressure releases, which cannot be covered in this book.

Toe ridge pressure releases work nearly the same way as do the pressure against the wall pressure releases. Let me first illustrate to you how I am drawing these toe ridge pressure releases. See illustration 44. Here in this illustration I have drawn an animal track that is planted firmly in the ground.

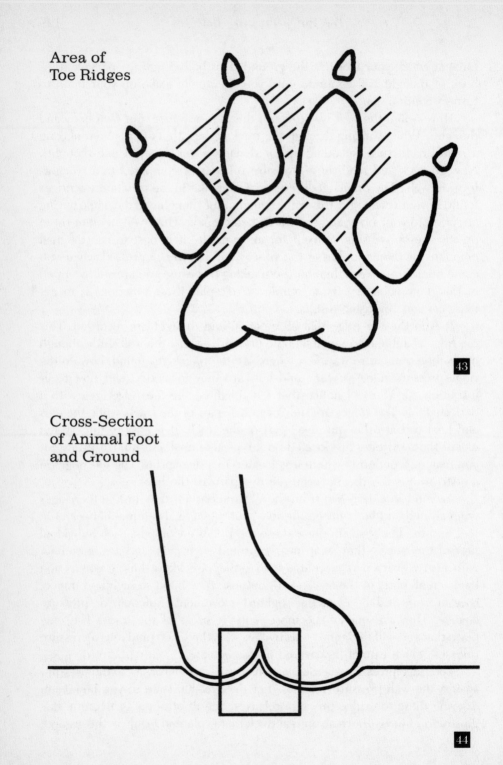

Area of
Toe Ridges

43

Cross-Section
of Animal Foot
and Ground

44

Toe Ridge Cliff

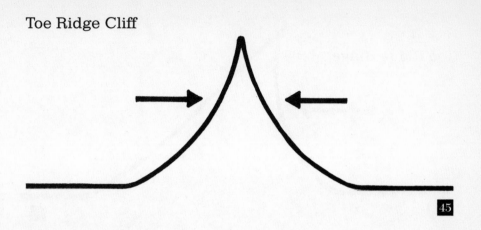

The toe ridge section, in this case the toe ridge between heel and toe, I have boxed in. It is what appears in this box that I will be using for my line drawing illustrations. Keep in mind that here I am drawing the toe ridge that separates the heel and toe. I could quite easily have also drawn two toes side by side and used that toe ridge. The end result would have looked the same.

Just as we did in the digital and lobular pressure releases, we must also put the qualifier "toe ridge" before the digital pressure release in order to define it. For instance: a toe ridge crest-crumble, with a secondary toe ridge ridge. Now let's move on to the first toe ridge pressure release. As you can see by the drawing in illustration 45, both sides of the ridge are sloped equally. This means that this section of the track had even pressure on the wall from both sides. This pressure release is called a toe ridge cliff.

Adding more pressure to one side of the track, you will observe a steepening of that side and a more dramatic sloping of the opposite side (see illustration 46). This pressure release is called a toe ridge ridge and it depicts the beginning of uneven pressure. You can tell which way an automobile is moving using the basics of this pressure release. The steep side is the direction the tire pushed, thus it is going in the opposite direction of the push.

In the next pressure release, the pressure side is hit with a little more pressure and intensity, but in a specific, pinpoint location (see illustration 47). This is called the toe ridge peak. Here the ridge has a high point, which depicts the highest pressure along that particular toe ridge. Now, if this sounds familiar to you, it certainly is. These, minus the qualifier "toe ridge,"

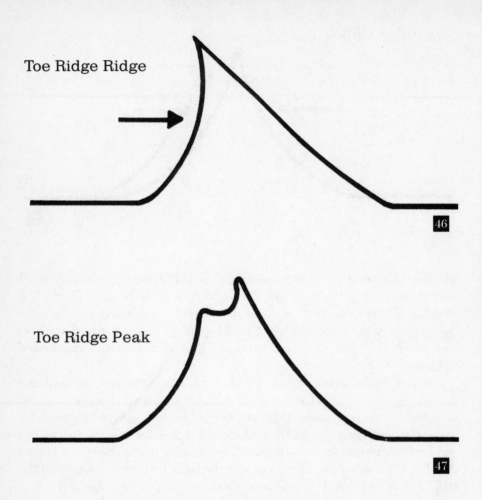

Toe Ridge Ridge

46

Toe Ridge Peak

47

are the names of the pressure releases for pressure against the wall. Essentially this is exactly the same force at work, only the wall is not a wall at all but a free-standing ridge. Remember, all earth moves in the same way.

Add more pressure and intensity to the ridge and the ridge begins to curve back toward the source of pressure (see illustration 48). This is called a toe ridge crest. Remember that the toe will rarely hit this crest upon exiting, for the same reason the foot rarely hits the crest as described in the pressure release study of pressure against the wall.

As we add more pressure to the toe ridge and crest, it can no longer bear up under its own weight. It crumbles into the track as soon as the toe exits (see illustration 49). This then is called a toe ridge crest-crumble.

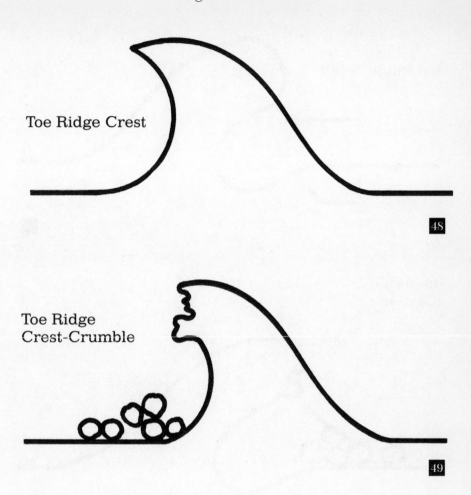

Toe Ridge Crest

48

Toe Ridge
Crest-Crumble

49

Remember that here the hyphen means the same as it has in all the other pressure release studies.

Just as in the pressure against the wall study, the toe moving downward produces a cave (see illustration 50). This, of course, is called a toe ridge cave; however, because it is in this very sensitive toe ridge area it tends to be more dramatic and undercutting than does a cave found on a typical wall. Remember, because the toe ridges are built up from loose soil, these kinds of pressure releases show up very well.

The next progression of pressure and intensity is obvious. The cave, due to intense pressure, load, and intensity, collapses into the track (see illustration 51). This is called a toe ridge cave-in. You will find that because of

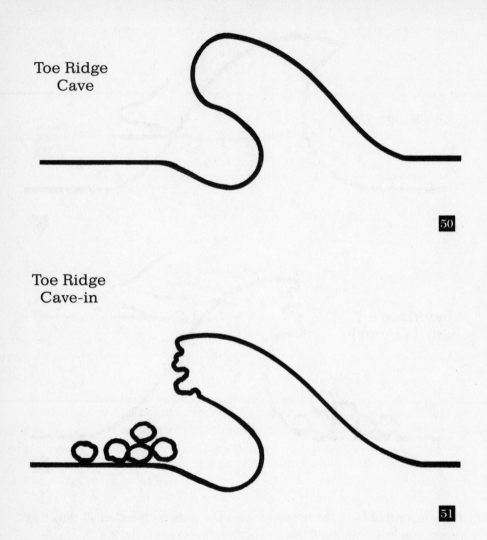

Toe Ridge
Cave

50

Toe Ridge
Cave-in

51

the personality of the toe ridge pressure releases and the pressure involved, it is rare that the toe ridge cave pressure releases occur. In fact, the following pressure releases are also quite rare. All of them combined are seen about 10 percent of the time, and even that number's a stretch.

Now the dramatic evolution of these pressure releases occurs. We cannot push into the wall with any more pressure, nor can we push farther down; the only option is for the pressure to move upward. The earth sheers off at the horizon and produces a plate (see illustration 52). This is called a toe ridge plate, but there is a problem in seeing it. Simply put, it is really

Toe Ridge Plate

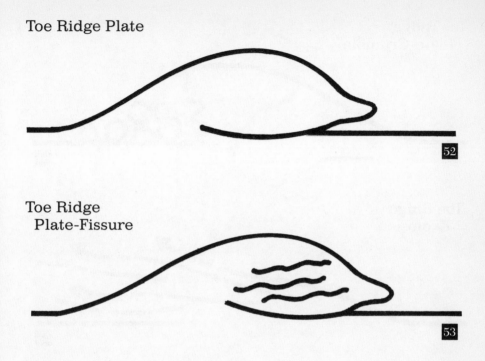

52

Toe Ridge
Plate-Fissure

53

small, incredibly small, for it rides right on top of the toe ridge. Most people would assume that the whole toe ridge will turn into a plate but this is not the case. To give you an idea of the size, in a bear print it is the diameter of a standard pencil eraser.

Just as occurred in the pressure against the wall, and knowing that all earth moves the same way, the next logical step will be a toe ridge plate-fissure (see illustration 53). Like the toe ridge plates, these are quite small and difficult to see at first, but with practice, and not much of it, you will see them with hardly a full hour of dirt time. However, the toe ridge plate-fissure and the toe ridge plate-crumble become even more obscure because the top of the toe ridge is typically broken up. Remember to look for the same size ratio as a toe ridge plate.

Next in the progression is the the toe ridge plate-crumble (see illustration 54). It is difficult to recognize because of the usually poor condition of the toe ridge top. It stands to reason again that this toe ridge plate-crumble will be as small and hard to see as any of the toe ridge plates. This is especially true when the track is well into the weathering process. In all of these plates, but especially the toe ridge plate-fissure and the toe ridge

Toe Ridge
 Plate-Crumble

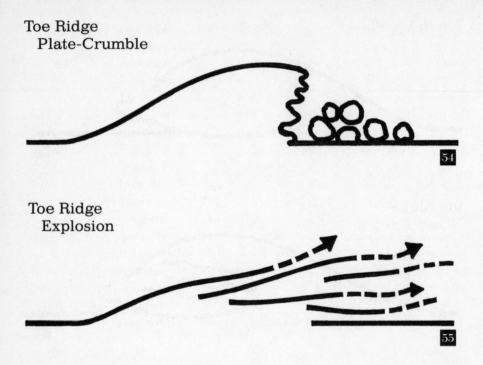

54

Toe Ridge
 Explosion

55

plate-crumble, reading through the damages of weather is going to take a lot of experience.

Finally, we have the toe ridge explosion (see illustration 55). This indicates maximum force from the portion of the track making this pressure release. Even when the track has gone through extreme weathering, the toe ridge explosion is easy to spot. An important note involving these toe ridge pressure releases is that the cliff, the ridge, the crest, the crest-crumble, the cave, the cave-in, and the explosion all involve the entire toe ridge, from top to bottom. However, the plate, the plate-fissure, and the plate-crumble involve only the uppermost portion of the toe ridge, i.e., the top. That is why they are so hard to read.

Now I want to discuss several very important concepts. The first has to do with shoes. I want to state again that all pressure releases, large or infinitely small, can be read right through shoes, boots, and any other modern footwear. But here we must push our limits of experimentation. They are very hard to see and very muffled, but with enough practice involving bare feet, animal tracks, and intense experimentation, you should be able to read the pressure releases through shoes within several hours. To reiterate, the more work you put into tracking people with bare feet, the easier it will be to read the muffled pressure releases through any kind of footwear. I have students, graduates of only three tracking classes, who are beginning to read the pressure releases through cross-country skis and snowshoes. Now that's three classes, each a week long, but these students have religiously put in their dirt time.

I also want to discuss deer and the other hoofed animals a little further. As I explained before, deer and other hoofed animals do have a toe ridge area. They also have a lobular area at the rear of the footprint, which itself tends to be lobelike in appearance. Deer can also produce the digital pressure releases. Each of the two hoof parts can be divided equally in half, with the forward half being the place of the disks and the rear half the place of the dishes. Each section of the deer hoof can and will work independently of the other. This is achieved because only the outside portion of the hoof and the contact edge is hard material. Inside this hard area is a relatively soft area that tends to be responsible for creating the digital pressure releases.

My final note has to do with the influence of weather on the toe ridges. Because the toe ridges are built high off the floor of the track and tend to be far less compact than the rest of the track, they are damaged by the weathering process very easily. You must take this into consideration when dealing with the track, for this toe ridge area will be considerably more damaged than the rest of the track will be. And quick damaging from even the mildest weather is going to hamper you when you try to read the toe ridge pressure releases.

The toe ridge pressure releases are the smallest and most definitive pressure releases outside of the macro and micro pressure releases. Practice with passion. Experiment with obsession. That is what is needed to understand these last two pressure release studies. You will find, however, that the first four pressure release studies will fall into place rather easily and with minimal practice and dirt time. Originally, I was only going to include the first four pressure release studies in this book, and was very confident that with just this information you would become a dynamic, master tracker. However, I knew that it would not be long before you would begin seeing lobular and toe ridge pressure releases and want to know why. Rather than ignoring them, or just giving you a simple explanation in just a few pages, I felt it necessary to give you as much as possible, leaving the rest up to you.

If you were now to count up all the pressure releases you have learned, you would find that you know 420 of them. You could go through the rest of your life practicing, experimenting, and putting to use these 420 pressure releases and never lack for anything. These will give you tremendous insight into an animal's very being. Yes, there are over 4,500 more, but those I have to teach one on one, face to face. I could never envision a book that would take you beyond these basic 420 pressure releases. The rest cannot be taught through a book, a tape recording, or even a videotape. You will just have to come to me. For now we will build on what we have done thus far, pushing beyond to create a greater, more well-rounded understanding.

12. INDICATOR PRESSURE RELEASES AND FOOT MAPPING

Through the wisdom of the pressure releases, we have at this point learned how to define the major and minor body movements, both internal and external, of an animal or human. We know how it moved in the larger sense, we know what smaller movements were involved in that motion, and we can penetrate right into the very core of the animal, reading the smallest movements and functions of the internal organs. The pressure releases are like words in an open book, a manuscript of life, that tells us everything about the entity we are tracking.

So, too, by using these pressure releases, we can precisely locate the next track, even before we see it. All of the wisdom of the next track and beyond is contained in the pressure releases of the track at hand. It is rare indeed that a master tracker will not know where the next track is located, or lose the trail, because of difficult tracking terrain. Master trackers observe tracks differently from everyone else. Our world of tracking is that of infinite detail and intense analysis. Our eyes become geared to the obscure, and in so doing, our ability to follow trails, even across solid rock, becomes as easy as tracking in sand. After all, we have become creatures of intense detail.

Another tremendous dividend of being a master tracker and reading the pressure releases is that we know exactly which animal we are tracking. In other words, we will never confuse the animal or human we are tracking with any other like animal or human. Many trackers have to rely on measurements to make sure they are tracking the right individual. But measurements are so variable due to weather and soil conditions, it is rare that we can measure beyond one-thirty-second of an inch, especially in the field. To put it bluntly, typical trackers often lose the animal they are tracking and get off on another trail, the trail of an animal similar in size to the one they were originally tracking.

INDICATOR PRESSURE RELEASES

The master tracker cannot mistake one animal's track for another's, because the master tracker knows—through the *indicator pressure releases*—exactly which animal or human he or she is tracking. This may sound like the beginning of a new pressure release study, but it is not. You already know the pressure releases that will become indicators. The best way to describe these indicator pressure releases is to define them as one would define fingerprints. Just as no two fingerprints are identical, according to the FBI, also no two indicator pressure release footprints are identical. Identifying and understanding the pattern of these indicator pressure releases assures the tracker that he or she is still tracking the same animal or human. There is no need for time-consuming, ineffective measurements.

So a master tracker, using the indicator pressure releases, knows the exact individual—human or animal—he or she is tracking, just as a law enforcement agent can attach an identity to a set of fingerprints. What's more, like the fingerprints, the indicator pressure releases will never change. You are born with them and they will remain with you forever. Thus you can locate a track and identify it as the animal you tracked a day ago, a year ago, or even five years ago. When another animal or human of like size, weight, height, and footprint crosses or merges with your trail, you will easily stay with the original trail you were following. The indicator pressure releases that the new, intersecting animal makes will be far different from the ones made by the animal you are tracking.

To define what is an indicator pressure release and what is not is actually quite easy. You already know what these indicator pressure releases will look like, because they are the same as you have learned through all six of the studies. The only differences are in their location and the redundancy of their appearance (they are always present). Typically you will find most of the indicator pressure releases on a digital, lobular, and toe ridge level. It is rare that you will find an indicator in the larger pressure release levels, such as pressure against the wall, changing and maintaining forward motion, roll, and head position.

An indicator pressure release is any pressure release on a digital, lobular, or toe ridge level, that is found redundantly, whenever that same track is made, and has nothing to do with the movement and function of the animal or human. In other words, the indicator pressure releases in the right front foot will always appear whenever that foot hits the ground, regardless of what the animal is doing in movement or function. Refer now to illustration 56. I have drawn this set of tracks as if the animal were moving straight ahead, where the right front foot comes down twice in the pattern.

As you can see from the illustration, I have drawn an eighth digital disk in the outermost toe of the right front foot. Each time that right foot comes down, that digital disk registers; no matter if the animal is turning right or left, going slow or fast, or any other internal or external function, that indicator pressure release is going to be there. Incidentally, I have oversimplified all of this in order to avoid confusion. Actually in each footprint

**Track Series
with Indicator
Pressure Release**

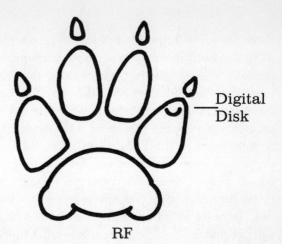

Digital
Disk

RF

LF

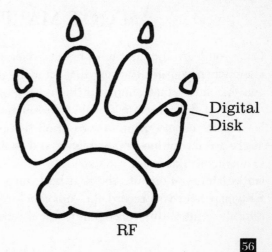

Digital
Disk

RF

there are a minimum of sixty-five indicator pressure releases, and the feet of no two humans or any other type of animal have the same set of indicator pressure releases. In fact, statistically, the indicator pressure releases are more defining and identifying than any fingerprint.

A typical question at this point is how one can tell if something is really an indicator pressure release or if it's pressure release caused by a function or movement of the body. In essence, that question defines the indicator pressure release even further. An indicator pressure release is not functional, meaning that it has nothing to do with, nor is it caused by, movement or function. All other pressure releases are caused by movement and function. In order to further prove you have an indicator pressure release, you will not find another pressure release that supports or corresponds with that indicator in any other part of the track. A functional pressure release has countless supporting and corresponding pressure releases that justify and define its existence.

The interesting thing about indicator pressure releases is that they occur in every conceivable tracking soil. Even on solid rock. Most of these identifying indicator pressure releases will register right through the heaviest shoes and even lug-sole boots. That is why they will become, very shortly, a valuable tool for the police. Gloves may hide the fingerprints but shoes cannot hide the indicator pressure releases. But more on this later. Right now all you have to remember is that indicator pressure releases are not functional and pressure releases are functional. And, like every other pressure release, these indicators can be found in all tracking environments and soils.

FOOT MAPPING

Once you learn the indicator pressure releases of an animal you will always know when you are tracking that animal again. It makes no difference if you encounter that animal an hour later or a year later. However, it is difficult at first, if not impossible, to remember the indicator pressure release patterns and combinations of all the animals and humans you track. There are far too many possibilities and similarities to be easily committed to memory. Since you can't really rely on your memory to identify these tracks later, you can use the next best thing, a foot map. Not only can the foot map help you record the indicator pressure releases of a human or animal for future reference, but it will also help you record special pressure release scenarios. Foot maps can also be used to convey precise information and detail to other trackers.

Refer now to illustration 57. You will note that for ease of understanding I have drawn the outline of a human foot. However, the basic grids that I use to map out this human footprint are also used to map out an animal's footprint. This one grid map, and the location principles associated with it, is used for all tracks, human or animal. All are done in the same manner. Notice that I have divided the human track in half so that it is bilaterally symmetric. I drew this vertical line—the vertical axis—by connecting the midpoint of the ball width measurement and the midpoint of the heel width measurement. The horizontal line simply marks the midpoint of the track's length, heel to toe; it is called the horizontal axis.

Now the track is divided into quarters, or quadrants. Each quadrant is identified by a roman numeral (quadrant I, quadrant II, quadrant III, and quadrant IV); this way you will not mix up the quadrant numbers with other identifying numbers used in the foot map. Illustration 58 shows how a typical animal track would look when foot mapped. Once the vertical and horizontal axes are found we can now begin to grid the track. Referring now to illustration 59, we have now divided the track further with forty equal horizontal lines. Line 0 begins at the toe, line 20 is the horizontal axis line, and line 40 is at the heel.

Now, in illustration 60, I have measured further and added in the vertical grid lines. This can be a little difficult to accomplish, especially because of the variety of shapes that can be found in the feet of both animal and human. Essentially it is quite easy, but because of the shape varieties, each quadrant must be measured separately. To accomplish this, measure the quadrant from the vertical axis to the outermost portion of the track. Now divide the quadrant equally with eight lines. Line A will lie closest to the vertical axis and line H will be the outermost part of the print. Each line is then lettered from A to H in each quadrant. Remember that each quadrant is measured independently of the others.

Right away you will notice the difference in the measurements. Illustration 61, showing the complete grid of a human track, will illustrate the different measurements and line location of the upper and lower hemispheres of the track. I use letters to identify these vertical lines so that there will be no confusion when relaying this information to another person. Vertical lines are lettered, horizontal lines are numbered, and the quadrants bear roman numerals.

Your initial drawing must be the same size as the actual track. This, as

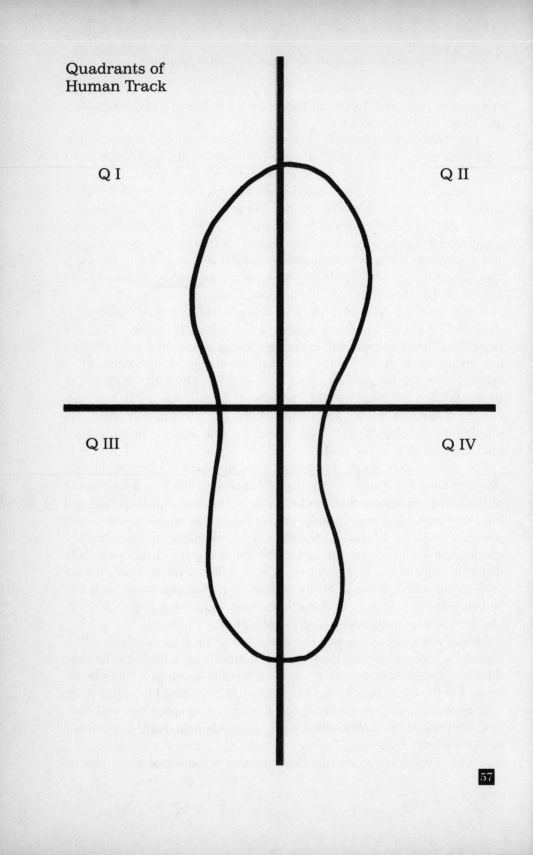

Quadrants of
Human Track

Q I

Q II

Q III

Q IV

57

Quadrants of
Animal Track

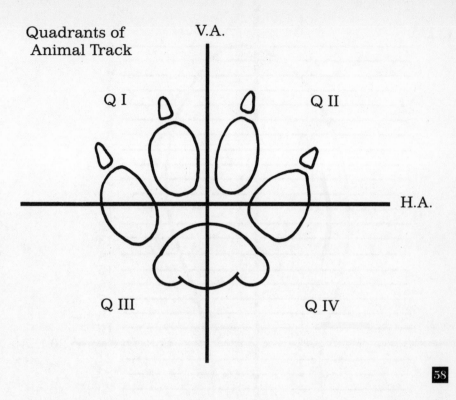

V.A.

Q I   Q II

H.A.

Q III   Q IV

58

you can see, is easy for a human track, but not so easy for animal tracks, especially very small animal tracks. If you drew small animal tracks' actual size you could not get all the line measurements drawn in without completely covering the track. This is solved by blowing the smaller tracks up in scale. Draw one foot of sketch for every one inch of track. Illustration 62 shows a mouse track drawn to approximately this scale. You can easily grid the track and convey all the information without crowding.

These track grids can then be used to preserve indicator pressure releases and their precise locations, or, for that matter, any other pressure release you want to record and preserve. For instance, referring to illustration 63, you will see that I have recorded three indicator pressure releases for posterity. In quadrant I, lines 13, 14, 15, and 16, and lines V.A., A, B, C, D, E, F, and G, I have recorded a small disk. In quadrant II, lines 3, 4, and 5 and lines A, B, C, D, and E, I have recorded a digital disk. In quadrant IV, lines 34, 35, and 36, and lines C, D, E, F, and G, I have recorded a heel pock. I could easily convey this information by radio to another tracking

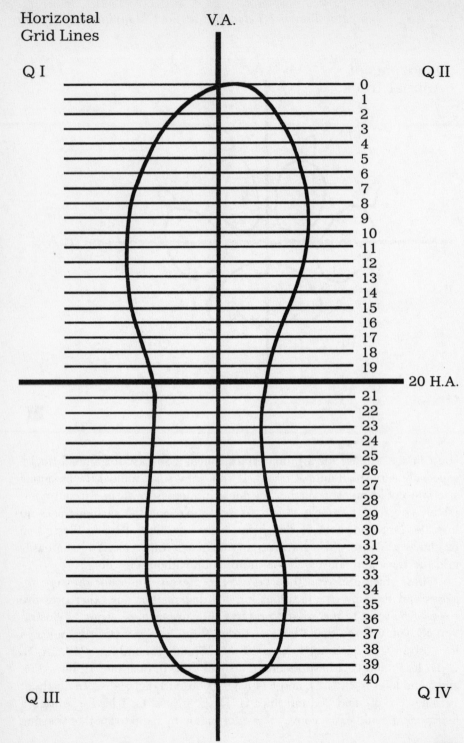

Horizontal
Grid Lines

V.A.

Q I

Q II

0
1
2
3
4
5
6
7
8
9
10
11
12
13
14
15
16
17
18
19
20 H.A.
21
22
23
24
25
26
27
28
29
30
31
32
33
34
35
36
37
38
39
40

Q III

Q IV

59

Vertical Lines

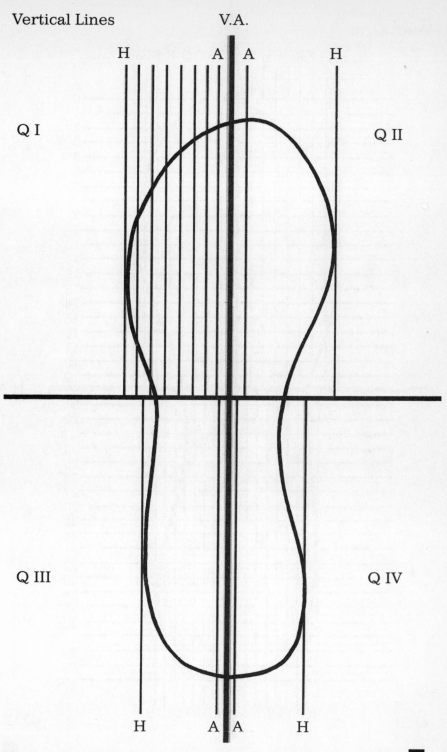

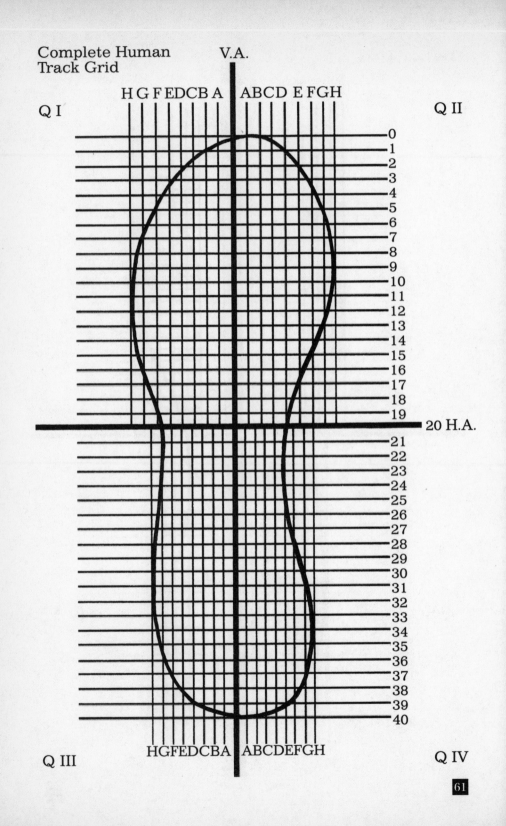

Complete Human
Track Grid

V.A.

H G F E D C B A   A B C D E F G H

Q I

Q II

0
1
2
3
4
5
6
7
8
9
10
11
12
13
14
15
16
17
18
19

20 H.A.

21
22
23
24
25
26
27
28
29
30
31
32
33
34
35
36
37
38
39
40

H G F E D C B A   A B C D E F G H

Q III

Q IV

Mouse Track Grid

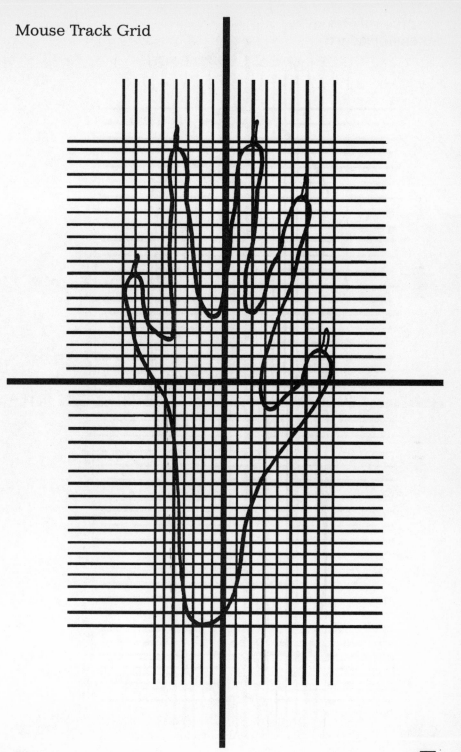

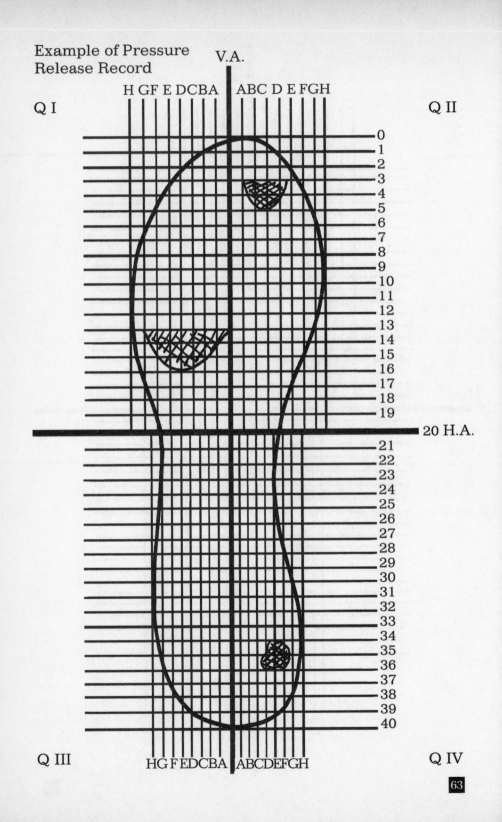

Example of Pressure Release Record

team many miles away. All they would have to do is to picture the track grid in their minds and they would know exactly where to find the pressure releases.

In fact, simplicity of communication is the primary reason that track gridding is done this way. Though it may at first appear daunting, it's actually quite simple. Everything from minus 1 and below is beyond the front of the track. Everything from 41 and up is outside the back of the track, and everything beyond H is outside the sides of the track. To record horizon data—changes to the ground outside the track boundaries—the track grids are expanded in this manner.

When I use foot maps and grids for a criminal court case, I go about the grid process in a slightly different manner. I first take a photo of the track, using a large-format camera, then I print the photo so that the track on the print is exactly the same size as the one found on the ground. I then overlay the photograph with a stiff sheet of clear plastic. All of my measurements and grid work are drawn right onto the plastic surface. Then I draw all indicator pressure releases I find on that same plastic overlay. This way, during the investigation or subsequent trial, the overlay can be flipped on and off the actual track photo. Needless to say, this then provides a clear view of the actual indicator pressure releases without the confusion of the grid map overlay.

Individual Track Analysis

Another good use for the foot map is in practicing individual track analysis. Actually, the grid is abandoned and we use only the actual drawn footprint, or series of footprints. Individual track analysis is one of the most important and effective practice techniques that we have at our disposal. It enables us to concentrate on all the pressure releases and then define their action in a very clear, easy-to-read manner. A single two-hour session of individual track analysis can take a tracker to a deeper level of understanding than a hundred hours of randomly viewing tracks can. Individual track analysis isolates, defines, and clarifies a track and its pressure releases.

The technique is very tedious and time-consuming, for it forces the tracker to look deeper into the track. At first it takes an average of four hours to properly go through the whole individual track analysis system. Eventually, with practice and dedication, all that will be accomplished with a fleeting glance of the track, once you have put in the dirt time. The full ramifications of this statement I will explain at the end of this chapter.

To do the individual track analysis exercise, you need a good artist's drawing pad, a little larger than a normal notebook; a ruler; an assortment of colored pens or pencils; and a notebook. You begin the individual track analysis as the name dictates: you find a good track, a single track. Now, lying down next to that track, draw the track onto your artist's sketch pad exactly as you see it in reality. Again, if it is a very small track, scale it up in your sketch pad. Once you have drawn the outline of the track, you are ready to go to work.

What happens here is that you are going to work your way through the pressure release studies as I taught them to you. Begin now by drawing into the track all of the primary pressure releases for defining pressure against the wall. Once these are drawn in, exactly as they appear in the real track, draw in the secondary pressure against the wall pressure releases. Using thin and thick arrows to indicate the kind of pressure and intensity needed to make each pressure release, analyze the pressure against the wall. This will tell you of direction change, slowing, stopping, and the other movements described earlier. Now record the result of the wall analysis in your notebook.

On the same drawing, indicate all the major changing and maintaining pressure releases found in the track, first the primaries and then the secondaries. Now analyze these for speed and forward motion, recording these findings in your notebook. Finally, using the same drawing and with shading to depict deep and shallow areas of the track, shade in the roll and head position pressure releases found in the track. Analyze this again and record the results in your notebook. No doubt you are now out of room in this drawing. Illustration 64 shows an example of a drawing at this stage.

Even if you have not crowded out your track drawing with pressure releases and arrow notations, it is best to draw the track again. This way there will be no confusing clutter. Next draw into this new sketch all the digital pressure releases. First the primary digital pressure against the wall, then the secondary digital pressure against the wall, followed by the primary digital forward motion pressure releases, and finally the secondary digital forward motion pressure releases. Again, using arrow notation, analyze and record what you have found. Here you will not only find evidence that will justify your major pressure release findings, but also information that will further clarify and define them.

Moving into the lobe section of the same drawing, record all lobular pressure against the wall, lobular primary and lobular secondary, then all the lobular primary and lobular secondary forward motion pressure releases.

Individual Track Analysis

Again, record and define what they mean. Finally, draw into the track all toe ridge primary and secondary pressure releases, analyzing and recording them. Now bring all of the pressure releases together and write down your overall analysis of that particular track. To justify or prove your findings you must find evidence of the movement in both the track that immediately precedes and the track that immediately follows your track.

Observing, drawing, and analyzing a track in this manner dictates a more intense and in-depth study. It forces the tracker to look for things that he or she might otherwise overlook. It builds theories about existing pressure releases that demand finer and finer details of justification, evidence, and proof. Thus, as the tracker builds a theory, the finer pressure releases are searched for and found to either back up that theory or tear it down. So too do the tracks just ahead of and behind the analyzed track.

All of this time and tedious effort to analyze one single track can become overwhelming and even discouraging at times. Try to keep in sight the end result. Learning the pressure releases is like learning to read a book.

The pressure releases are like letters of the alphabet; the pressure release combinations become words, and the tracks become manuscripts. When you learned to read, you would stumble across the "big" words, but after seeing them time and time again you could eventually read them with ease. So too with the pressure releases. Patterns of pressure releases repeat themselves quite often, and by learning them this way, you will one day be able to glance down at a track and read the entire manuscript.

What once took you hours to accomplish will now be accomplished in a glance, but you have to pay your dues. The dues of dirt time, of tedious scrutiny, practice, and experimentation. In tracking, and especially in pressure releases, there is no other way. The pressure release pattern that took you four hours to analyze today will only take you an hour of analysis tomorrow, a few minutes of analysis the next day, until ultimately only a fleeting, knowing glance is needed. Then the pressure release patterns will have become words, just as the letter combinations of the alphabet eventually did.

13. SOIL PERSONALITY

Throughout this book I have repeatedly told you that all soil moves the same way. *Soil* seems to be a term that can be broadly interpreted, but most people think of soil as the kind of dirt found in a garden. I prefer how Grandfather put it: that all *earth* moves in the same way. However, to me, the term *soil,* like *earth,* is still far too limiting. I think the statement should really be that all tracking mediums, all tracking surfaces, move the same way. That takes in all possibilities, from rich garden soils, to the leaf litter on forest floors, to gravel, and even to the dust and grit that is found on solid rock and floor surfaces. This broader interpretation, which encompasses every tracking medium, is exactly what I want you to understand.

Pressure releases occur everywhere, no matter what the surface, no matter what the conditions. They occur in the sand of the tracking box, the soils of the field, the gravel beds, the forest litter, the lawns, and on solid rocks. The more difficult tracking situations do not limit themselves to the larger, more dramatic pressure releases, either, for even the smallest of pressure releases are recorded there. So too do these pressure releases remain readable even when severely weathered. Certainly the wind and weather conditions work to erase the tracks, and certainly the smaller pressure releases are fragile, but they do hold up far longer than people usually imagine.

You have probably already begun your soil comparison experiments and are now beginning to understand its intricacies. That is, providing you have divided your tracking box into three different compartments and started your experimentation with those three different soil conditions. (Refer back to chapter 8, if necessary.) Unfortunately what I now must tell you to do is what I've told you to do with pressure release studies 4, 5, and 6, and that is to *study and experiment.* However, I can make your dirt time a little more productive, especially in the area of soil personalities.

You must understand that the division of the tracking box is critical to your soil experimentation. What happens in the three compartments of this box—containing the normal, damp sand, the dry sand, and the hard sand—forms the baseline for all other tracking mediums. In other words, no matter what the mix, the composition, the adhesive qualities, or any other personality of any given medium, its behavior can always be traced back to the basic movements found in the three tracking conditions of the tracking box. That is why it is so essential that you study, practice, and experiment with the divided box, before taking the soil personality analysis actually into the field.

In my Expert Level Tracking classes, students learn that there are 107 different soil combinations and factors—107 distinct personalities they must explore and understand. There is no way that in the scope of this basic book I can articulate and thoroughly explain those 107 possibilities; however, I can group them into what I call sectional soil personalities. These fewer sectional possibilities make understanding the overall concept easier and make the topic a manageable one for this book. From these sectional soil personalities, with dedication and experimentation, you will eventually be able to make further divisions yourself and eventually arrive at the 107 soil personalities I teach to the more advanced classes.

Let's now begin to look into several of the major soil characteristics that must be first defined and then thoroughly understood. Refer now back to the divided tracking box. In the compartment where you prepared the sand by dampening, raking out, then lightly smoothing and pressing—in other words, the normal, damp sand—you will find that this sand's personality reflects the behavior of 80 percent of all tracking mediums that you will encounter in the natural world. This then becomes the most important box that you should study. Here is 80 percent of all tracking soil personalities you will encounter, and to know how the sand moves and reacts in this box is to know most of the personalities in the natural tracking environments.

In the compartment containing the dry sand, you will find that this sand reacts the same way that 10 percent to 15 percent of the soils in the natural world react. In the final compartment, where the sand has been pounded so hard you can barely register a track, you will find that this pertains only to about 5 percent of the natural tracking mediums. These three basic tracking box divisions contain the overall personalities of how all tracking mediums will react to movement, function, and pressure. Eventually, once you work your way through the expanded sectional personality categories described in the following pages, you will be able to connect them back to the original tracking box conditions.

Adhesive Quality

Adhesive quality of any given soil is one of the most important characteristics of soil personality. The adhesive quality dictates not only how soil will cling or stick together but the personality of the pressure releases it will build. Much of a soil's adhesive quality is due to water content, which remains the most important factor. Lesser factors are the microbial content of the soil, the soil type, and the amount of impurities. Soils with low water content react much like dry sand, while those with high water content react like normal tracking box sand. Subsequently, the first thing you should do is determine what the adhesive factor or quality of the soil is, even before you begin tracking.

To experiment with the adhesive quality of the soil, take a handful of soil from close proximity to the track, making sure that the soil conditions there are nearly the same as that of your track. Grip the soil firmly in your hand, compressing it together as hard as you can. Then release your grip and watch how the soil in your hand reacts (see photos 29, 30 and 31). If it falls apart easily, then it has low soil adhesive quality. If it fissures or crumbles under its own weight, then it has medium adhesive quality, but if it holds together well and does not crack or drop bits of soil, then it has high adhesive quality. Actually these are only three gradations of the soil adhesive quality index. There are twenty in all—twenty different gradations, thus twenty different soil reactions. But those are part of the further breakdown into the 107 soil personality categories. All I want you to consider right now is the basic soil adhesive quality.

Duration of Adhesive Quality

Here is a further refinement of the adhesive quality index. Through experimentation it teaches us how the adhesive quality breaks down. Some soils lose their adhesive qualities quickly while others hold onto that quality long after they dry out. Furthermore, the poor adhesive quality of drying soil will mean that the pressure releases made when the adhesive qualities were high will cause those pressure releases to fall apart easily, while soil with a high adhesive quality will maintain perfect pressure release formations long after the soil has dried out.

To further illustrate how this kind of experimentation is done, you will have to make several tracks in the same area, all containing large pressure releases. It is best to make these tracks when the soil adhesive quality is at its highest. As the soil dries, you come back to the area every hour or so, grab the soil from next to the track, and compress it in your hand. This will help you to determine the diminishing characteristics of the soil's adhesive qualities. During each visit for soil compression analysis, check the condition of the existing pressure releases and see how they are drying out, how they are holding their shape, or otherwise reacting to the drying process. Of

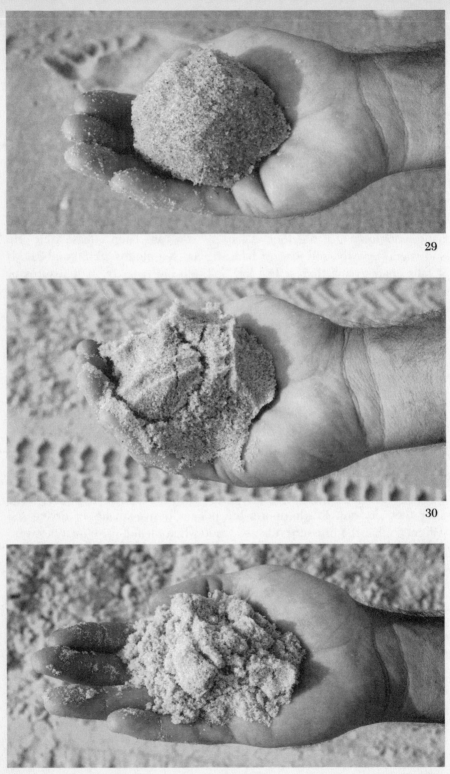

29

30

31

course you will have to do this in many kinds of tracking soils and mediums. This is essentially what I mean by impassioned and dedicated experimentation. It means lots of time and work.

Water Content

In discussing analysis of soil adhesive quality I mentioned the importance of water content as the major factor contributing to adhesive quality. Some soils need little water content to be adhesive while others need to be nearly saturated to have the same adhesive qualities. Also a consideration is the water-holding duration of a soil—how long a soil will hold its water in various weather conditions. This is important not only to the proper aging of a track, which we will discuss near the end of the chapter, but also to pressure release formation. Also along that same line of analysis and experimentation is exactly how a soil dries out. Does it dry out evenly or in a varied state, and how fast does it dry out? All of these things must be taken into consideration.

Density

Density of a soil means how tightly the soil is packed together. Low density means that the soil will "give" easily, with little resistance, much like dry sand. Medium density means that the grains of soil are more tightly packed and will "give" less easily and hold together a little better, just like the normal sand of the tracking box. And high density soil means that the soil has low "give" characteristics, meaning that it will react like the hard-packed sand of the tracking box. However, almost immediately in your soil experimentation you will find some soils that have high density yet will throw pressure releases like you would find in the dry sand tracking box. Again, words of explanation cannot substitute for even five minutes of experimentation and study.

Mixture Quality

This area of consideration is very important and equally difficult to begin to understand, especially considering all of the variables. Mixture quality simply means the "impurity content" and "distortion index" of any given soil. Mixture quality, impurity content, and distortion index are all related and all affect the way that the final pressure releases are formed. Sand that

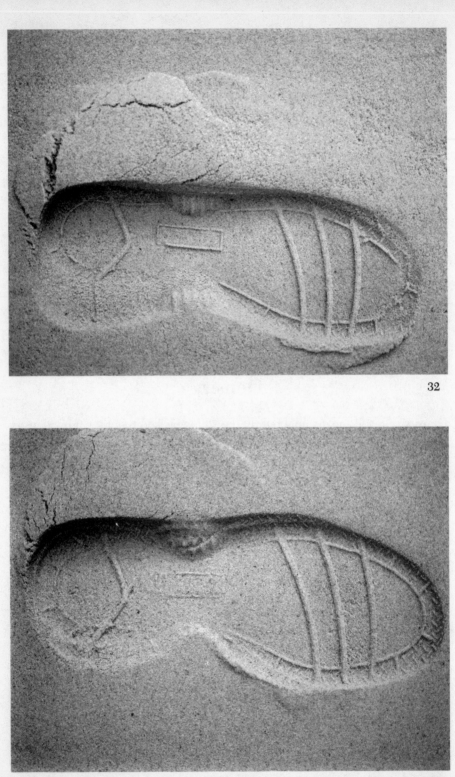

32

33

contains a few larger grains has a low impurity content, while deep forest loam or forest debris has a high and quite variable impurity content. Generally, the higher the impurity content the more likely the distortion, which means that the pressure releases will be distorted forms of the originals. Low impurity content promises minimal distortion while high impurity content means that the soil has major distortion possibilities.

The distortion index can be explained in this example. Given sandy soil with a low impurity content of a few small stones, you will find that a plate will "crack" along these stone areas, throwing a minimal "landscape-imposed distortion." The same plate thrown in deep forest debris will "crack" along all of the debris and thus throw a maximum amount of "landscape-imposed distortions." Here, when dealing with mixture quality, you must take into account the impurity content and the distortion index, determine the amount of landscape-imposed distortion, then identify the precise pressure release. A badly cracked plate may at first be mistaken for a plate-fissure, but by determining the distortion factors you can define it as a plate. This takes experimentation and experience. More on experimentation will be found at the end of the chapter. Photos 34 and 35 show two examples of mixture quality.

Pressure Personality

This is the way that a particular tracking medium, or soil, reacts under pressure. Sometimes the pressure reactions are quite startling, defying logic, by reacting contrary to what you might think. For instance, some tightly packed soils of high density will have a lot of give on the track floor, but not on the track wall. Some soils may be spongy, where the elasticity factor of the soil causes it to bounce back. Such a pressure personality is usually directly proportional to the amount of soft debris mixed in with the soil. It is not only the debris mix, but also the "memory" of that debris to return to its original shape.

Experimentation and testing are accomplished by pressing on similar soils and watching for elastic spring-back potential. Some of these soils even have a delayed spring-back, coming back up slowly over a long period of time. Elastic factors and sponginess account for that. Some track floors do not spring back under normal conditions, but when bathed in rain or even dew, they swell like a sponge with the added moisture. You can further test this pressure personality by compressing a clump of the earth in your fist, then releasing the pressure and watching the movement of the clump as it

34

swells and returns to its original form. From this test you realize that the pressure releases, not only on the floor, but also on the walls, will be affected in the same way.

Building Capacity

How much, how high, how thick, how broad a pressure release will build in a certain soil is an important concept in the soil personality study. Different building capacities can produce considerable variations in the pressure releases for the same movement. Here in building capacity, so many soil personality categories, and countless combinations of soil personalities, come into play. Reaction in one type of soil can produce vast differences in the resultant pressure release thrown, confusing differences. In "zero" soil (sand), the resultant pressure releases will be the same, but in the wild, to the untrained eye, they appear to be different. This is simply because the untrained or inexperienced tracker does not take into account the landscape-imposed distortions that would justify the vast differences. Knowing these differences would, in the final analysis, produce the same end result.

Gaining experience with the building capacity of the pressure releases in the various soil personalities requires an ongoing experiment. This takes little setup or preparation; you can practice it anytime you take a walk. Decide on a particular pressure release you want to use during a particular outing. It's best not to concentrate on more than one on any given outing at first. Let's say that your first experiment concerns an extreme turn to the right, from 12:00 to 1:30. In your tracking box this would produce a typical plate-fissure. Now memorize this exact movement and degree of turn, using your tracking box, until you can duplicate that plate-fissure every time.

Now take that movement and bring it into the field. As you walk along exploring nature and following tracks, take time out to duplicate that same movement in all types of soils you encounter. Then closely scrutinize the results. Watch the building capacity of the soils and how different they look at first. Then search for the similarities between all the tracking soils, discounting, of course, the landscape- and impurity-imposed distortions; these similarities will telegraph through the dissimilarities. Suddenly, with an accumulation of practice, these pressure release building capacity personalities will be seen in a new light.

Shape Identity

The compression shape or the "shape identity" characteristics of the pressure releases are closely associated with the building capacity; they, too, have more similarities than differences, and it takes experimentation and practice to know the differences. You can practice learning shape identity at the same time and in the same way that you do the building capacity similarity identification. In this way, too, you can study something called the holding capacity—that is, how long a pressure release lasts in a particular soil in a variety of weather conditions. This demands a frequent return to the pressure release during weather events, bringing many personality characteristics together.

Landscape Location

Another influence in the soil personality can be its location. You must take various landscape locations into consideration when experimenting. Tracking soils differ dramatically from one location to the next. The most obvious example would be to compare a track in a well-exposed area to a track in a more secluded and protected area. The differences during weather events would become obvious. A track found on a slight hill would drain water faster than one located in a lowland. You may well test some soils and find them to be of the same makeup and personality, yet find also that they behave differently due to where they are found.

Aging Characteristics

The personality of any given soil will greatly influence how the pressure releases break down during the aging process. Each soil personality has its own aging personality also, which, of course, must also be taken into consideration during experimental exercises. In my book *Tom Brown's Field Guide to Nature Observation and Tracking* I lay out a detailed plan for effectively teaching oneself how to identify the exact age of a track. In abbreviated form, it is this: Go to a prepared rectangle of soil, one that has been freed of all debris. Using the rounded end of a broom handle or a deer's foot, make five marks in a line. Incrementally increase the depth of each succeeding line so that they vary from ¼" to 1" deep. As soon as the marks are made, record the time and the weather conditions, then carefully scrutinize these fresh marks, committing the finer details to your subconscious mind.

At intervals of six hours, come back to the box and make another set of marks, right alongside the last and at the same depth. Again record the time and weather conditions. Now scrutinize the fresh marks and compare them to the older marks, committing all to the subconscious. Why the subconscious? Because trying to define the nuances of degradation would be beyond words or any logical explanation. This process should be kept up for twenty-four hours, and repeated several times, many times. Eventually, when you've gained enough experience with the six-hour intervals, you should graduate to one-hour intervals, then half hours, then every fifteen minutes. In doing this time after time, with soil after soil, in weather condition after weather condition, your ability to age a track becomes both exact and effortless.

The condition of the lateral ridge is one of the most important features of the track to look for to help determine age. You may want to review the beginning of chapter 6, where I introduced the "true track." The lateral ridge, you will recall, is the line along which the floor of the track and the wall of the track meet. They do not form a right angle as most people would expect (see illustration 65a), but, given the spread and drag characteristics of the foot, where they meet appears as a very thin ledge running around the track. See illustration 65b. As you can see from this illustration, this is not a right-angle meeting, but a sweep-type meeting that terminates in a little shelf.

It takes quite some doing to see this lateral ridge; that is why most people see and measure tracks only from the "overall track" perspective. To give you an illustration of how small this lateral ridge is, let's discuss the size in a human track. Considering that the lateral ridge, through cross-section, appears like a small shelf, imagine a human hair lying on that shelf. The hair would overhang that shelf by quite a bit (see illustration 65c). Isolating and identifying the lateral ridge will take some doing on your part. You have to look at the track in a different way. See the lighting enhancement techniques discussed in chapter 14 for a more detailed discussion of this positioning technique.

Once you have spent enough time in the manufactured track aging boxes, it's time to graduate to realistic conditions. In this case you would watch an animal make a fresh track, scrutinize it carefully, take down the time and weather conditions, and then return every half hour to watch its progress. Each time you return to that track you should put a fresh mark

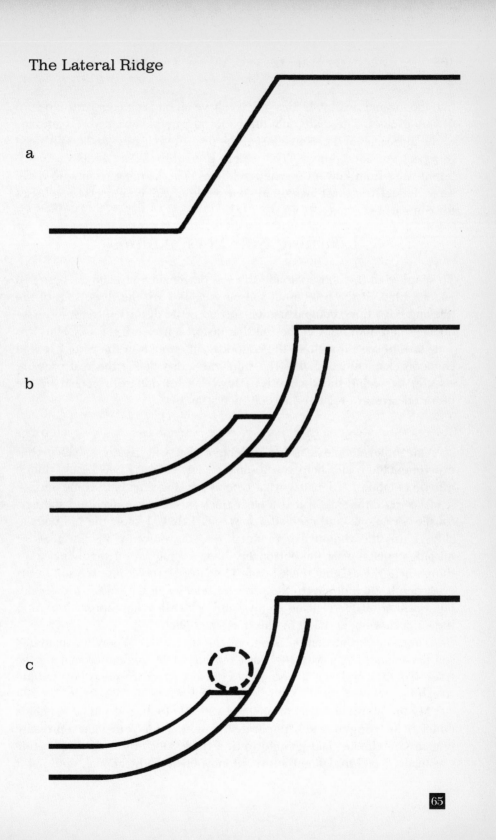

The Lateral Ridge

a

b

c

into the ground nearby. In this way you have an ongoing comparison record of various ages. These are only the basics of aging knowledge. To advance to the intricacies and personalities of the pressure releases you literally need to repeat the same process. The various pressure releases age in vastly different ways from how an overall track does. The learning technique is the same, except you must include in your marks a variety of pressure releases for comparison.

Learning Soil Personalities

To simplify all the above variables in soil personality, remember these two factors: First, at the base of all soil personalities are the three soils of the tracking box's three compartments. Second is the distortion factor—the influences and impurities in the soil that distort a pressure release. Thus it is your task to see through all the countless differences in these soils to find common characteristics. It is the similarities that define the real pressure release; by seeing the similarities you will learn not to be fooled by the distorted pressure release that first meets the eye.

One other simple learning technique that will greatly enhance your experimentation, and help you to analyze any track, is one I call "thumb experimentation." No matter what type of tracking situation I come upon— it makes no difference if it is a clear track in sand or a distorted soil personality situation—and no matter how well I think I know the soil personality, I use the thumb experimentation. This prevents any mistakes or misjudgments in what soil personality I am dealing with. I simply place my thumb near the existing track I want to analyze, press it into the soil to the exact depth, then duplicate the pressure releases of the track with a bending, pushing off, or twisting of my hand. Thus the thumbprint duplicates the exact movement made by the track (see photo 36).

Thumb experimentation is one of the best ways I know for analyzing soil personality along with the exact movement of the animal making the track. To Rick and me, it became a critical part of learning the pressure releases.

My thumb became one of my most valuable tools. I would lie for hours on my belly trying to exactly duplicate the motion it took to make a pressure release Grandfather had pointed to in a track. Once the *exact* duplication was made, I had to define the overall movement of the animal, then put it

into some frame of reference, some order of ever-increasing pressure. If I ever dared venture to ask Grandfather a question, he would only answer by asking another that was designed to lead me to the truth. It was a very long, detailed, and meticulous process that took an intense level of awareness and observation. Just defining one pressure release could sometimes take us an entire week of study, sometimes even more. To further complicate things he would give us the pressure increases out of order, pointing to midpressure zones instead of starting from the beginning.

There is no way around it. I could never conceive of trying to give you every variable, every soil personality, every little detail of the pressure releases in clearly defined language. Even if I could write an entire encyclopedia of information I could not convey to you the half of it. There is no replacement for experimentation, keen awareness and observation, dedication, and the passion to learn. It has to be done if you ever hope to master tracking as Grandfather defined the concept. Read this book and with just a little study, you will be great, but you have to give it your all if you want to be a master tracker. That is why the next chapter is dedicated to the concept of practice and experimentation.

14. EXPERIMENTATION AND EXERCISES

Since I have repeatedly stated that experimentation, practice, impassioned need for learning, and keen awareness skills are so paramount to the understanding of the pressure releases, I have decided to dedicate an entire chapter to this subject. Certainly I have given numerous examples of experimentation techniques throughout the text, but a more comprehensive treatment will fill the gaps. Subsequently, I have outlined several experimental methods and considerations in the following text, but the list is in no way exhaustive. It is meant only to lay a basic foundation of experimental discipline, which can be expanded upon as the tracker's skill grows.

Continual practice and experimentation should be happening every moment of every day, no matter where you work or play. Foremost in your mind should always be the questions "What happened here?" and "What is this telling me?" This constantly questioning consciousness, which should become a habit, will demand answers and the answers will demand an intense searching and a keen sense of awareness. In the context of this "questioning drive" alone, there are people to study, actions and reactions to observe, and movements to scrutinize. After all, among the more important initial study subjects are humans, including yourself.

For instance, when riding a subway or a bus on your way to work, look at the wear marks on people's shoes; observe what they observe and what they ignore; become conscious of how they react, with body language, to any given situation. This constant scrutiny and awareness of people should carry over into the work environment and even into your own home. If you are driving, there are countless landscapes, traffic patterns, and other drivers to observe. There are bits of trash, tire marks, broken-down vehicles, and myriad other things that need answers, deep answers to those constant questions. City or suburb, wilderness or park, there is always a constant source of wonder, of questions, that need to be answered.

Besides the all-important constant questioning of the tracker consciousness, one must also develop the habit of constant experimentation and practice. I call it a habit, for it must be an unconscious act, something that goes on all the time without thinking, and not an act that you must prepare for in advance. No matter where you go or what you do, you must be constantly experimenting with soil personality, how the various pressure releases react, and every other conceivable experimental study that comes to mind. It makes no difference if this experimental study is in the silence and isolation

171

of the pathless woods or in a patch of dirt in an abandoned lot of a city. Constant experimentation must be both a natural, effortless act and an on-going quest.

Reading the Hard Surfaces

Let's begin now with the basics of learning to read tracks and pressure releases on the hard surface environments, such as floors, stones, and solid rock faces. The Scouts were always known for their ability to track anyone or anything across solid rock, much to the amazement and disbelief of out-siders. In fact, to almost all of the best trackers throughout the world, track-ing across solid surfaces remains impossible. Yet, by following a few basic rules, understanding the concepts, and taking the learning process one step at a time, you will immediately begin to see these tracks. With just a little practice you will begin to see the pressure releases.

The basic rule of reading tracks on hard surfaces is to *keep the track between you and the source of light*. In the beginning especially, it is ex-tremely important that you do this. A second "must" is that you view the tracking surface from an extreme angle. In order of importance, the light source relative to track location is the first priority while the extreme viewing angle is a distant second. Once you grow accustomed to viewing these tracks using these techniques and have amassed many hours of experience with them, you will be able to abandon the extreme viewing angle first. With more practice you will eventually see the track no matter where the light is coming from.

Try this dramatic illustration. First find a floor that hasn't been cleaned or dusted in several days. The floor also has to have a window at the far end, so that you can look across the floor toward the window opposite you. It is also best to have some sort of overhead light that illuminates the floor from above. Now, with the window curtains closed tightly, allowing in no light, sweep your foot across the floor in a huge, arching "S" curve. Then, from the far end of the floor, with the overhead light turned on, look at the floor. You will see tracks.

Now turn out the overhead light, open the window curtains, and view the floor from the end opposite the window. Because you are at the far end of the floor you are already looking at the floor surface from a severe angle. What you will see now is that the floor seems to flare up, dramatically revealing the track. It is startling to see such a spectacular change. As you move back and forth along your end of the room, you will notice the track's "flare" change personality and intensity as the angle between and the light changes. Walk now to the window side of the room and look back across the floor: the track will have disappeared. The track is no longer between you and the source of light.

Let's now consider how this track will appear to you—for tracks on hard surfaces have two distinct personalities. If the overall surface of the floor is dull, then the track will appear shiny; inversely, if the overall surface personality of the floor is shiny, then the track will appear dull. This rule holds true for all hard surfaces, whether it be a floor or one of the many rock and hard ground situations you will encounter in a natural setting. So, no matter what the surface, you first define the personality of the overall surface as dull or shiny, then you will know if the track will be shiny or dull.

To add more challenge to the floor experiment, lightly sweep the floor of all tracks. Now walk across the floor, moving back and forth as you go. Then repeat the viewing process, first looking at the floor with the overhead light on and the curtains drawn, and second with the overhead light off and the curtains open. You will see each step appear perfectly as a shiny or dull footprint. Graduate now to your pet dog or cat. Sweep the floor again and allow your pet to wander from one end to another. Then view the floor with the changes of light again. Though these prints will be smaller, they will still stand out in a very striking manner.

Showing this to the officers during a police or S.W.A.T. team class, I give an even more sensational demonstration. Two hours before I plan to have the officers do this exercise, I mop and wipe down the kitchen floor of an empty house and seal off all entrances. Then two hours later I return and walk across the kitchen floor. Keep in mind that the house is totally empty and the kitchen sealed off. The officers are amazed at the high visibility of these tracks even after just two hours of allowing the dust to settle. Imagine the kind of dust and grit that would be found in an open outside environment. Even after a heavy rain, there is enough grit left on the hard surfaces to define tracks beautifully.

Tracks found on a hard surface, like a floor, are called *dust and grit compressions.* In illustration 66a, you will note that the hard surface is covered by a light covering of dust and grit particles. These particles cover all surfaces, indoors and out. Whenever anything steps on the floor (see illustration 66b), the dust and grit are compressed into the floor. The flattened dust is then facing upward. Depending on the personality of the

Dust and Grit Compressions

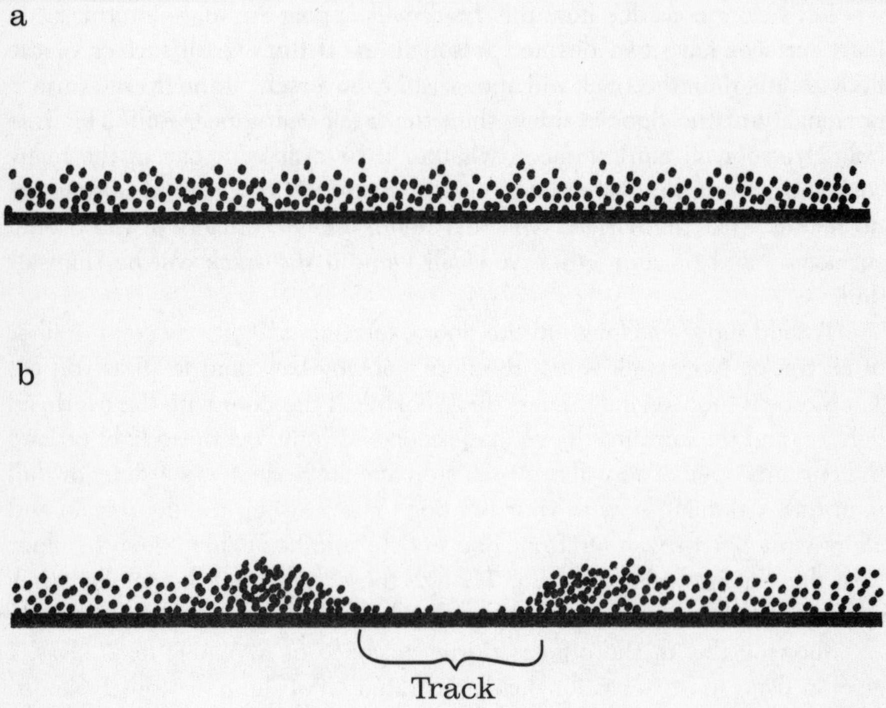

a

b

Track

66

surrounding floor and the overall condition of the dust, this flattened re-flective surface will have either a dull or a shiny reflective personality.

We have so far been viewing these tracks from across the floor; often, however, you will need to achieve that severe viewing angle to look at closer tracks. For that you have to use a technique called "sideheading." To side-head closer tracks you must lie down next to the track and put the side of your face directly onto the ground. Then, opening the lower eye and closing the higher eye, you are able to view the tracks at a severe angle from your eye to a few feet away. Closing the lower eye and opening the higher one allows you to maintain the severe angle of observation from a few feet to several feet away. After that you must slowly lift your head off the ground to view the more distant tracks.

Many students assume that because these dust and grit compressions are made of such light material, they must get swept away quickly by the processes of aging. Let's examine this concept using the bigger world. Let's say it has snowed six inches and when the snow ends late in the day, you track through it to go out and feed the birds. Later that night, two more inches of snow falls on the existing snow, and of course on your tracks. The next morning are you still able to see where you walked in the snow to feed the birds? Of course you are. The snow has covered everything equally, and the depressions of your tracks, though softened and muffled, are still quite apparent. So it is too with the subsequent settling of new dust and grit on your tracks and the overall tracking surface. You can still make out the depressions for quite some time.

Lighting becomes a problem when the sun is directly overhead or the sky is overcast. It becomes almost impossible to get that track between yourself and the source of light. The only recourse you have, until you gain enough tracking experience not to need the light source location again, is to use a small flashlight. Even on glaringly bright days, a small but powerful flashlight placed at the opposite side of the track will give you enough angular light to be able to see the dust and grit compression. However, I recommend that at first my students track when the sun is at a low angle to the ground—usually in the hours between dawn and ten A.M. and between four P.M. and dusk. This lower position of the sun will allow you to move around the track so that you can place it between yourself and the light source. We'll have more on this in the next section, "Night Tracking."

There are several easy experiments you can do anytime to enhance your ability to read tracks on hard surfaces. First, select a dead leaf from a tree. This way you will be assured that it has never been stepped on; you can also be assured that it is well coated with dust and grit. Now carefully lift the leaf up so that it is between you and the source of light and observe the personality of the leaf's surface. Now very gently touch the surface of the leaf with the tip of your pinky, with less pressure than the foot of a mouse would deliver. Hold the leaf up again to the light; suddenly the pinky print will flare. In fact you will be able to see some, if not all, of its fingerprints.

Again, if the overall surface of the leaf is dull, then the print will appear shiny. If the overall surface is shiny, then the print will appear dull. Now try the same experiment with a small rock. Select the rock from a protected location, not along a small animal trail, so that you can be assured that it has not been recently stepped upon. Repeat the above exercise and you will observe the same dramatic results. Try this same experiment with many different "hard" objects, such as pieces of wood, shreds of bark, stems of plants, fragments of glass, or anything you can think of. If you think that the print is caused by the oils of your hands staining the surface, then try the experiment with cotton gloves or even surgical latex gloves. They will produce the same results.

You have seen how dramatic a light touch of the pinky can be on the hard surfaces that you have experimented with. Well, isn't a leaf surface, a rock, or a piece of wood like a hard floor to a mouse? Of course it is, and a mouse will use a lot more pressure than you used in pressing with your pinky. So use this same method for tracking on a forest floor strewn with debris, or a gravel bed strewn with stones, to track a mouse or other small animal. Simply, if the animal is not heavy enough to compress the tracking medium he is walking upon, he is still certainly heavy enough to compress the dust and grit on the surface of that tracking medium. Subsequently, you can track him easily.

You can also now use the same methods of sideheading and light position to locate and define precisely a track's lateral ridge, which marks the true track. In fact, at first this is the only way you will even see it at all. That is why most people use the "overall track" measurement method, for that is all they have the capability to see. To define the lateral ridge keep the track between you and the source of light and view it from up close, using sideheading. Look at the overall personality of the track. If the overall track is dull, then the lateral ridge will appear as a thin, shiny, hairlike line. If the overall track is shiny, then the lateral ridge will appear as a dull hairlike line. As I stated before, with practice you can see it directly without sideheading or keeping the track between you and the source of light.

Night Tracking

In the last section, on reading tracks on hard surfaces, I made the statement that it is best to track when the sun is at a low angle to the ground. The usefulness of the sun's position goes beyond just reading the compressions on hard surfaces, however, for any tracking is better when you keep the track between you and the source of light. It makes no difference if the track is on a hard surface, a gravel bed, in forest or field litter, or even in sand. To position yourself so that you are looking toward the source of light always dramatically enhances any tracking surface. Essentially, with the sun or source of light at an angle, you have shadowing of the tracks, and thus a striking depth to them. If the sun is directly overhead, the ground appears washed out, lacking depth and shadow.

In night tracking with a flashlight, you may find that you become a better tracker, contrary to what logic would tell you. After all, you control the angle of the source of light, thus the shadow and depth of the tracks. I have found that certain colored lights work well in very specific environments. White, or clear, light works well on clear ground, gravel, sand, and for most other open-ground tracking. It is also the best for all hard surfaces. Red light seems to work best for forest floors, illuminating the debris, or litter, without glare or washout. Yellow light works best for grasslands and lawns, while blue light works best for snow and ice conditions. Even my students who are color-blind note the remarkable improvement these colors make for viewing the various environments.

You can purchase many of these colored lenses with the better brands of flashlights, but some colors are just not manufactured. You can get the standard military-type flashlight, for example, with a clear, a red, and sometimes a yellow lens, but rarely blue. To manufacture your own color filter, buy color plastic in a hobby shop and simply wrap the plastic over the end of the flashlight, holding it in place with a rubber band. Incidentally, for nighttime color photography it is best to use these same color filters on your flash attachments. I found out when I was older what colors work well, largely through personal experience or from my students who experimented with light sources. Grandfather made us track with a torch and would not permit any other source of light.

Try this experiment for learning how to night track with the use of a flashlight. Late in the evening when the sun has long since set and you are surrounded by full dark, find an open patch of ground that has been traveled over a lot. An open, much-used hiking trail will work well for this basic experiment. Holding the flashlight high overhead, point the beam straight down at the ground so that the beam is perpendicular to the trail. You will clearly see that the ground appears washed out and very few tracks are visible. Now turn off the light, hold the flashlight parallel to the ground, about a foot above the surface, and switch on the beam. What you now see is breathtaking, to say the least. The ground erupts with all manner of tracks, even tracks that you could not see during daylight hours.

Now lift the flashlight beam up and down, keeping it always parallel to the ground, and watch the track shadows deepen and diminish with each movement. The higher up you go, the smaller the shadow; the lower you go, the deeper the shadow. Now experiment by tilting the beam slightly toward the ground, raising and lowering it again. Here you will find even more changes. Moving the beam from side to side will produce more changes still. What you want to do is to get to the point where the beam hits in such a way that it reveals the best tracking visibility. Now try standing with the light pointing at the ground, the same way most people would use a flashlight. Notice that the tracks nearly disappear. That is why people don't usually do night tracking. They just do not know how to hold the flashlight at a useful angle.

To further experiment with the capabilities of the flashlight and the subsequent control of shadows, give the flashlight to a partner. Have him or her move to one end of the trail and shine the light back toward you, horizontal to the ground. This puts the track between you and the source of light. Now, not only will you note the shadowing and depth of the tracks, but a new dimension will be added. You will begin to see the shining and dulling of the various tracks. Of course, this should be the method you use when tracking over solid surfaces. After all, there are very few and faint shadows on solid surfaces and what you want to reveal is the contrasting shine or dullness of the track compression.

Once you have experimented with the various angles and degrees of track enhancement in this open trail area, it's time to move on to grasslands, to lawns, to forest debris, and any other kind of tracking environment. Here the same amazing changes will occur with the movement of the horizontal beam. So too will it take a little more experimentation to find the best viewing angles for the tracks. Too much shadow and everything blends together, too little and you do not see the track at all, and unless you get the light beam perfect there will be far too many distracting variables. Each situation presents a new set of circumstances—hardly any two like soils can be read the same way with a flashlight. That is why, as you follow tracks at night, you have to keep the light beam constantly moving and changing, meeting the challenge of each new terrain as you go along.

Blind Tracking

Back in the first chapter that dealt with pressure releases—chapter 6, about pressure against the wall—I made a bold statement. I said that if you studied the pressure releases of the track before you, then you will know exactly where the next track lies, even before you find it. Like Grandfather said,

"All the wisdom is in the last track." One of the major parts of Grandfather's training was to blindfold Rick and me, then have us follow a trail. He wanted us to develop a touch sensitivity to the pressure releases, and subsequently be able to find the next track, but he also wanted us to be able to track at night if we ever found ourselves without a torch. Naturally he was not satisfied with having us follow tracks in easy soils; we had to do it in all soils. Even across solid rock.

One thing Rick and I would practice all the time is what we called "canvas tracking." Rick would lay a long narrow sheet of canvas over a series of animal tracks while my back was turned. He would erase all visible tracks before and after the canvas sheet except for the one that lay immediately before it. This way I would not have any clue as to what the animal had done before he got to the canvas or after his trail went beyond. I would then study the visible track carefully and identify the next track location from the pressure releases. I then pushed a straight pin through the canvas and into the ground beneath, where I thought the track would be located. Eventually we abandoned the canvas tracking because it became nearly impossible for either of us to miss the next track in any tracking medium.

This remains one of my favorite beginning tracking exercises. You do not need a canvas sheet. Any old piece of cloth will do. Have a friend lay it out over a trail, leaving you only one track. Study the track carefully then push the pin through the cloth. If you successfully hit the next track, roll the cloth back down and continue on. If you fail, find out why; define in your mind how you misread the pressure releases so that you will not make that mistake again. Grandfather once said, "Nothing is a failure, as long as we can learn from it," and that is especially true of tracking. Simply stated, failure teaches!

Once you become good at canvas tracking, make your goals higher. Using a blindfold and a soft delicate touch, begin to follow animal tracks wherever they lead. Go faster and faster and push yourself through all types of terrain. Never be satisfied until you can track almost as fast blindfolded as you can with your eyes open. Going further, feel out the large and small pressure releases with your hands. Describe what you are feeling to a friend and have him draw a foot map based on your description. Your partner should also take a picture of the track so that you can compare the picture to the drawing later on. Remember that touching the track will eventually destroy the pressure releases and it is difficult to compare the foot map drawing to a fingered track.

Because of the effectiveness of feel-tracking I have never turned away a legally blind person from any of my classes. My blind students can easily learn tracking as well as their sighted counterparts. In fact, one of the best trackers that I know of is totally blind. At first he had a little difficulty with tracking concepts, but never with following trails. In fact, I have sent him out on several tracking cases with my Tracker Teams, and in two instances he was instrumental in finding the lost person. He has become an asset to any tracking team, for in conditions where the eyes fail, like night tracking, or when the eyes can play tricks on you, he excels and leads everyone else.

Debris Compressions

Before we start experimenting with debris and getting into the dynamics of reading pressure releases in it, let's begin by describing what a debris compression is. Debris, first of all, is the litter of the forest floor or the matter found covering the ground in a field. It is made up of decaying leaves, bits of seed, shreds of bark, wood and plant fibers, tiny fungi, little plants, insect parts, grass stems and fibers, and all manner of other materials that carpet the floor of forest or field. It lies in layers of progressive states of decay; the fresher materials are on top, the various seasonal strata are below that, and underneath all is the decaying loam, where the individual debris particles have virtually lost their identity.

This carpet has a loft, a fluffiness, that is generally uniform (see illustration 67a). A tracker following a trail through a debris area first establishes the natural loft or height of that debris. Once the personality of the debris is identified through its loft, the tracker knows that anything pushed, dented, or compressed into that debris is a track (see illustration 67b). You might think that because of the resiliency of debris, it will eventually work its way back up to its original height. This is just not the case. Not even with the most resilient and supple of debris material. There is simply always some sort of a compression to be found.

What happens to debris upon compression is well illustrated by a common household carpet. You know that vacuuming a carpet lifts its fibers to a natural loft. If you step on a vacuumed carpet, you can easily see your footprints sunk into it. Whenever you move furniture that has been on a rug or carpet for a long time you can see the compression marks the feet or the base made. This is exactly what happens in the debris found in the forests or fields. When animals step upon it, the debris is compressed, and

a

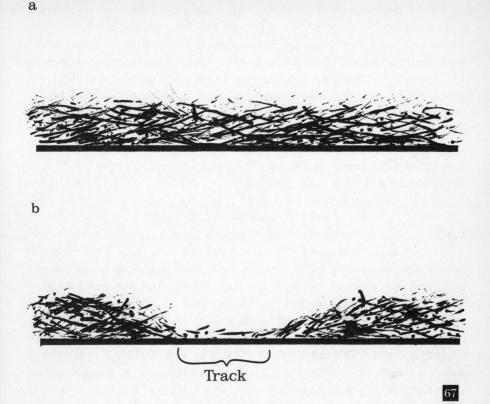

b

Track

67

a compression mark is left behind. As stated before, the lighter animals, such as mice, that are not heavy enough to leave a compression can be tracked as if on hard surfaces.

Pressure releases are also found in this debris. Many novice trackers believe that since the debris is not made up of soil, it cannot create a pressure release. This is wrong, so wrong. The debris itself creates the pressure release; the debris works together and moves to produce the pressure release. What is left, then, is not simply a dent in the ground of uniform depth and dimension. Instead, it is obvious that the debris stacks, builds, moves, and reacts in much the same way any soil does. To define this similarity you clearly have to practice, experiment, and compare. There is just no way around it. Another note is that debris pressure releases are not just the larger pressure releases but also the smaller ones, and even the eighths divisions.

Many people, especially those with a little dirt time, can understand the formation of the pressure releases on the uppermost layer of debris. These reactions, however, are not confined to the surface. Reactionary pressure releases are also seen at many levels into the debris and beyond. Evidence of the uppermost pressure releases are not only identified, but proven and justified, at the lower levels and far beyond. No track begins or ends at the compression point. In other words, the track does not end at the floor, walls, horizons, and all the other visual places. Instead, the track is like the center of a concentric ring, a ring that ripples well beyond and under the existing track. To illustrate this rippling impact, let's look at the next example.

Layer Cake Analysis

This experiment dramatically illustrates the effects a track has beyond its parameters. To prepare for this analysis, you need a cardboard box two feet long, one foot wide, and at least ten inches deep. You also need a bag of white flour and a pail of dark soil that is free of all impurities, such as stones, sticks, and other debris. Place the box on the floor and fill the bottom of the box with two inches of soil, smoothing it out evenly, then gently packing it down with a small board. Next, add a layer of flour to the top of the soil, about one-eighth of an inch deep, smoothing it so that it is of one thickness and covers all of the soil, right to the ends of the box. Now carefully add a half inch of new soil, covering the flour, smoothing it evenly, and packing it gently. Repeat this process so that there are at least eight layers of soil and seven layers of flour. See photo 37.

Once the box is complete, take a step into the box, turning and pushing off slightly as you walk through. This movement, of course, will create a plate, a dish, and possibly even a secondary disk. It makes no difference the kind of pressure release you end up with but you want to keep the movement small and simple, nothing dramatic. You want to produce pressure releases on the floor and on the walls. That is why I make this movement suggestion. Now carefully cut out one side of the box, the longest side, using a sharp knife and being careful not to jar or disrupt the box as you cut. Once the side has been cut out, it will reveal the corresponding dark and light layers you have created, much like a layer cake in appearance. This, of course, is where this experiment gets its name, although Grandfather had us use ground calcite or powdered shell instead of flour.

37

Using a sharp twelve-inch ruler, begin to peel away the earth a little at a time, as though you were taking a thin slice. Use a downward cutting motion, and take care not to hack or disrupt the inner layers of the box. Pull all excess dirt toward you and push it out of the way. This way you will have a clear view of what distortions the layers have gone through. Now as you cut closer to the track, you will notice that the rows of flour are beginning to wave a bit; some are buckling and showing erratic lines. Yet you will still be several inches away from the track. As you cut further back, you will find an ever-increasing disruption in the lines. They buckle, break apart, wave, swirl, and go through all manner of contortions. Yet still you will be outside the actual track imprint.

Finally as you begin to cut into the track you will notice the most dramatic changes yet. Many of the flour lines are horribly bent, some are broken off, others are not only fractured but located several inches higher or lower than the rest of the line. So too will you notice that the contortions of these lines reach out far, not only to the outside wall of the track, but also deep beneath its floor. In most cases the disruptions, compressing, and violent contortions of the lines reach right to the box bottom. This obviously shows that a track's "concentric rings" reach far beyond and beneath the original track parameters. This is the same with tracks in all natural tracking environments.

It is obvious from this simple experiment how far-reaching the impact of a track extends. Here you can see formations in the flour-soil mix identical to many of the larger geological formations around you. Here too you can clearly see how the rippling effects of tracks are very much like water in their movement. Viewing the ground much like a liquid greatly enhances your understanding of how tracks and pressure releases move. Keep in mind when doing this experiment that you should only cut through and remove a little soil at a time. I vary my cutting from around a quarter of an inch in the outer areas to an eighth of an inch for the intricate movement areas; thus, all the cross-sections are thin.

This layer cake experimentation should not be something you do only once. It becomes a valuable tool in understanding pressure dispersal, pressure release formation, and the rippling effects of tracks. I suggest strongly that you use this layer cake method to fully understand the underlying influences of all the larger pressure releases. It will help you to know how the soil reacts not only on the surface, but also beneath the surface. I also advise you to eventually add small stones and parts of twigs to the soil, thus to learn how these impurities influence and possibly distort pressure releases from deep beneath the surface. Layer cake analysis gives you the whole picture both above and below the surface. It allows you to observe realms that very few others have ever thought about, far less seen.

Another basic concept that you will begin to notice with the layer cake analysis is that all pressure releases that are found on the surface of the tracks have components in the subsurface layers. In other words, each layer will have evidence of the above pressure release. This holds true not only in this obvious layer cake prepared soil but in all soils as well. The most obvious place to see this phenomenon in the natural environment is in forest or field debris. Here you can see the subdebris reacting to the major pressure releases, subsequently validating their existence. This same interaction of the subsoil to the surface pressure releases can be found in all other tracking soils but it is very difficult to identify, far less see, unless you have the experience.

We can now apply what we learned from the layer cake experimentation to tracks found in debris. Find a debris compression that has several well-formed pressure releases in the debris. Refer to photograph 38. Carefully remove the upper level of debris until you hit the damper, more decomposed lower level. Here you will clearly see evidence of the larger pressure releases you found on top of the debris. Remove more debris until you hit a level of loam, where the debris has all but lost its identity. Here in this rotting sublayer you will note further evidence of the upper pressure releases. These sublayers of debris will hold not only the track for a long period of time, but also the pressure releases found in and around the track. The debris acts as a natural weather barrier and the aging process can take months to erase a track here.

Several other experiments can help you to understand how feet react and form pressure releases. When I was first learning the pressure releases, I thought it would be great if I could see up through the ground as something was walking by. To see the feet move as they made contact with the ground I thought would help me fully understand the process of building a pressure release. I decided to pay a visit to a local wrecking yard and get an old back window from a pickup truck. I placed the window between two sawhorses and sat underneath, then I watched Rick walk back and forth. The reaction of the feet as they ebbed and flowed with pressure was astounding. We used that old window for years, learning so much more than I could ever put into words.

Eventually we grew older and heavier, until the window glass could no longer take my weight and I broke through. However, the importance of

that experiment could not be overlooked. Today I have a steel frame from an old glass table. I replaced the glass with a sheet of laboratory-grade Plexiglas, which is about three-eighths of an inch thick. Though it is not as clear as glass, it is still a tremendous teaching aid for my advanced tracking classes. I strongly advise against using glass of any kind if you are going to do this on your own. Make sure the Plexiglas you use will more than support your weight. I have found that you do not need to use a steel frame, but can build an adequate frame from two-by-fours. The best would be a frame that is four feet long by two feet wide and far enough off the ground for someone to lie down underneath.

Another way to get a real feel for the way dirt moves is to step slowly into firm mud. You will feel the mud move beneath your feet, much like water, as you walk, turn, or go through any other normal movement. The firm mud essentially reacts the way all soils react, though in mud it is much easier to feel the "give" of the surface and subsequent flow of the pressure. The feeling of the mud moving beneath your feet gives you an idea of how soil reacts to the various pressure you exert. I tend to view all soils, all tracking mediums, as more of a liquid than a solid. This way it is easy to understand how soils flow into pressure releases.

Functional Experimentation with Pressure Releases

It is time to say it again: If you are going to be a master tracker then you need a passion that borders on obsession. And that passion needs to be fed with relentless experimentation and keen observation and awareness. You must learn to enter the passionate consciousness of a master tracker, whereby you constantly observe and experiment no matter where you are. People, domestic and wild animals, and all of life's situations must come under your constant scrutiny. You must watch the subtle movements, actions, and reactions of all things and then connect those actions and reactions to the tracks and their pressure releases. There is just no way around this passionate experimentation and observation, for no amount of words or demonstrations can teach you the finer intricacies of the tracks.

During my childhood, when I was first beginning to experiment with the pressure releases, I used myself and my dog as sources of study. This allowed me a certain degree of control over the tracking environment, the conditions, and other variables. I knew that my own pressure releases under specific conditions would be very similar to my dog's, and my dog's pressure releases would be similar to all other animals'. After all, my bare foot had digits, toe ridges, and lobes that would produce nearly the same results as would be made by the rest of the animal world. Thus, using my own tracks and those of my pet dog became my doorway into the rest of the tracking realms.

I would do the following experimentation, and variations of it, with myself and my dog. For instance, I would not eat anything for twenty-four hours and then walk through my tracking box, knowing that my stomach was completely empty. I would then eat a good meal and immediately go back to the tracking box and walk right next to the original, "hungry" tracks that I had set down earlier. I would do the same with my dog. Then I would compare the two sets of tracks, noting the differences between the stomach full and stomach empty pressure releases. This side-by-side comparison would become the basis of all study. From the outset, I found that this was the best and easiest vehicle to mastery.

I would do this same side-by-side study—in my tracking box, using both myself and my pet dog—for bladder full and empty, awake and sleepy, tired and rested, thirsty and watered, sick and healthy, injured and healed, and countless other physical conditions. Always the side-by-side experimentation and comparison would beautifully illustrate the differences and variables. Once the extremes were understood, like stomach full or empty, I would then study the increments of fullness. For instance, I would not eat for twenty-four hours, then walk through the tracking box, then I'd eat a little, walk through again, and study the results. I would then eat some more and repeat the process time and time again until I was completely full. This way I could tell from the pressure releases the exact amount of food I had in my belly. I would then do the same with my dog. Eventually, I did the increment study with all body functions I could.

After mastering these subtle pressure releases in the controlled environment of the tracking box, I moved to the variety of landscapes and tracking surfaces found in the natural environment. I repeated the same process as in the tracking box and still used myself and my pet dog as the study subjects. Once I mastered these side-by-side comparisons in all soils from sand to gravel to deep forest litter and all the others, I then moved on to more advanced experimentation, observation, and analysis. As I mentioned earlier, I would watch a deer defecate, then go over to where it relieved itself, study the tracks before and after its scat, then make the comparison. I followed feeding animals, scrutinizing their tracks as their bellies grew full, watching the differences growing in increments.

I did this comparative analysis with all animals, scrutinizing each track for evidence of function and movement, in all possible tracking conditions. Simply, I would watch an animal carefully, note exactly what it was doing and when, then go over and compare the tracks. I did this time after time, with animal after animal, in topography after topography, year in and year out, until I mastered the tracks. The journey to understanding the tracks is both relentless and never ending. There is just not enough time in one life to exhaust all of the subtle possibilities. Yet, the journey to mastery is always exciting, always rewarding, and always an adventure.

The Pressure Releases of Thought and Emotion

Yes, emotion and even thoughts can be read in the pressure releases. Here again you must use yourself as the first study subject, for you intimately know what you are feeling and thinking as you make the tracks. By first studying yourself, you then become a vehicle to understanding the emotion and thought pressure releases of all other people and, subsequently, for all other animals. In essence, the process is the same as you used for the functional pressure release experimentation described above. You need the same side-by-side comparative analysis, only this time instead of comparing the function you are comparing thought and emotion.

I accomplished this study of thought and emotion by first knowing, intimately, what my tracks looked like when I was feeling and thinking normally. Then when I became angry, depressed, worried, frightened, joyous, confident, or any other emotional condition, I would walk through the tracking box and compare the tracks. What is surprising is that the differences are quite startling and dramatic. I also repeated the process with thoughts. I would begin to walk through the tracking box then think of turning right, but still maintain the straight ahead movement. Here again I would study the track where I had the "turn right" thought, and compare it to the others. Again the differences were dramatic. You would think they'd be very subtle or even imperceptible, but, in the final analysis, these thoughts and emotions have a surprisingly powerful impact on the pressure releases.

It is important to remember here that your thought and emotion pressure releases are very similar to all other people's and in fact to all other animals'. The only problem is that it is a little more difficult to know what an animal is thinking or feeling as he makes the tracks. That is why your pet dog or cat is so instrumental in this study. You can better know what your pet is thinking or feeling, thus your pet can become a vehicle to understanding all other animals. Again, you need keen observation and awareness skills, especially when dealing with emotion and thought.

If all of this seems impossible to you, then let me ask you this. Do you walk the same when you are happy and confident as you do when you are extremely depressed or worried? Of course not. Your physiology is quite different in the two extremes. When you are depressed, your shoulders are drooping and forward, your head is tilted downward, and you walk as if you have the weight of the world on your shoulders. Yet when you are happy, your head is held higher, your shoulders back, and there is a certain bounce to your step. The same physiological changes and variables hold true for all emotions, thoughts, and bodily functions. The more conscious you are of these subtle changes in your tracks, through intense self-analysis, the more dramatic differences you will see in the pressure releases.

Advanced Tracking Boxes

Since we are on the subject of experimentation, practice, and analysis of tracks, I will now suggest, strongly, that you add several other tracking boxes to your collection. These can be small boxes, one containing gravel, another containing forest loam and leaf litter, and a collection of other boxes that have mixed soil types. This way, once you graduate from the basic tracking box you can study subtle pressure release differences in these other tracking boxes. Thus you can study soil variables in a controlled environment. Yet there is no substitute for the natural world. The tracking boxes just make it much easier to make the transition. Nonetheless, to this day, I still use my tracking boxes, especially when I come upon a new concept where intense comparative analysis is necessary.

❖ ❖ ❖

Again, intense experimentation, awareness, observation, and passion are the keys to unlock the door of mastery. There is just no way around it. If all you do is read this book and apply some of the major principles of pressure releases you will be a good tracker. But if you want mastery, if you want to read the Earth as Grandfather did, then you will need his passion.

15. FURTHER REFINEMENTS OF THE WALL STUDIES

Now that you have a firm foundation in the basics of pressure releases, we must move forward and expand upon the pressure against the wall pressure releases. This expansion allows the tracker to further divide wall pressure into precise increments, much like you learned for the changing or maintaining forward motion pressure releases. I have purposely waited until late in the book to expand these wall pressure releases, for it can seem too subjective and become far too confusing at the onset of the teaching. In essence I needed to make sure that you have had some experience before going forward with a more precise incrementation of the wall pressures.

Basically, the wall pressure releases are further divided into eights increments, much as the disks and dishes of the forward motion pressure releases were divided. However, not all of the wall pressure releases are divided in this way. Only the ridges, the peaks, the crests, and the plates have these further divisions. The crest-crumble, the cave, the cave-in, and the explosion pressure releases will remain as you first learned them. These are just far too subjective to divide further. Yet, with experience, you will see even a major difference with these latter pressure releases. It is also important to keep in mind that when the primary pressure releases are divided into eights, so too are the secondaries. Thus the secondary ridges, peaks, crests, and plates will follow the same incremental divisions.

Eighth Ridges

To the experienced master tracker it is no longer acceptable to define a ridge as merely a ridge. Ridges come in sizes that reflect precise increments of pressure. Basically, ridges are measured in eights, with the larger the ridge, the greater the pressure. In other words, ridges are measured in proportion to the depth of the track. To keep it simple, let's say that a track is one inch deep, from its floor to the horizon. If the ridge rises one-eighth of an inch above the horizon it is called an eighth ridge. As it grows taller it then becomes a quarter ridge, where the ridge is one-quarter of an inch tall. It will then go to a three-eighths ridge, a half ridge, a five-eighths ridge, a three-quarters ridge, a seven-eighths ridge, and finally to a full ridge. A full ridge is as tall as the track is deep. See illustration 68.

To further explain the correlation of ridge size to track depth, we'll now say that you have a track that is two inches deep and a ridge that measures one quarter of an inch in height. This is not called a quarter ridge but an

Cross-section
of $^1/_2$ Ridge

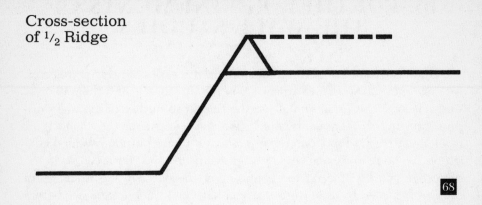

68

eighth ridge, because one to eight is the proportion of the height of the ridge to the depth of the track. It should be noted here once again that each soil condition has its own personality. A ridge that would build to a half ridge in certain soils may only build to an eighth ridge in other soils. This differentiation will become clearer as you experiment with the various soils and how they build. However, all you have to remember at this point is that the higher the ridge, the more pressure was exerted against the wall.

Eighth Crests
Crests are also measured in eights, the same as the ridges, in proportion to the depth of the track. And, like the ridge, the taller the crest, the greater the pressure against the wall. Thus you have eighth crests, quarter crests, three-eighths crests, half crests, five-eighths crests, and so on. Remember that the crests are incremented and defined exactly as the ridges are.

Eighth Peaks
Here again the peaks are measured as the basic ridges are. If a peak stands alone then it is incremented and divided in the same way as the ridges. If a peak rides on a ridge (as they most often do), then it is described as, for instance, a quarter ridge with a three-eighths peak. In other words, the peak is one-eighth of an inch taller than the ridge, given that the track is one inch deep. See illustration 69.

Eighth Plates, Plate-Fissures, and Plate-Crumbles
The plates, the plate-fissures, and the plate-crumbles are all incremented into eights. Here again, the larger the plate, the more pressure that was

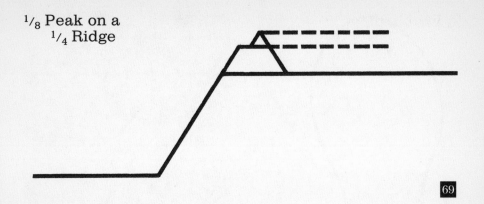

$^1/_8$ Peak on a
    $^1/_4$ Ridge

69

exerted against the wall in any given soil type. However, plates are not measured in proportion to the depth of the track, but to the proportion of the width of the track. See illustration 70 and photo 39. You will note that in illustration 70 the plate is exactly one-quarter the width of the track; the track this depicts is four inches wide and the plate is one inch wide. Whereas in photo 39, the track is four inches wide and the plate-fissure is two inches wide, thus it is a half plate-fissure.

If the plate is thrown off the front of the foot, such as when the animal or human is slowing or stopping, the plate is measured in proportion to the length of the track. In illustration 71, for simplicity's sake, let's say the track is eight inches long and the plate is one inch long. Thus the plate is called an eighth frontal plate.

To further define where you should measure the width of the track as compared to the width of the plate, it is important to establish a centerline on the plate. You will note in illustration 72 that the plate falls in the second quadrant of the foot map. Measure the plate down the middle and measure the width of the track at the point where the line intersects the wall, as shown by the arrows.

A convoluted plate is one in which several different areas of pressure work against the same wall section. For convoluted plates (see illustration 73), you must treat each convolution separately. The convolutions are numbered. Plate convolution #1 lies closest to the toe, plate convolution #2 is the next, and plate convolution #3 is closest to the heel. As you will note in the illustration, a centerline is drawn from each convolution and track width is measured from that centerline at the point where it meets

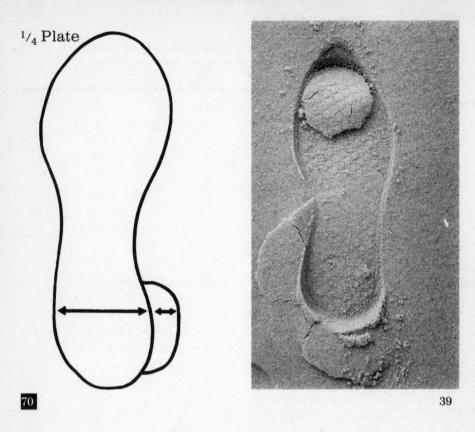

¹/₄ Plate

70

39

the track wall. Thus you will have three measurements for this convoluted plate.

When you begin to study eights in pressure against the wall, I recommend that you use a ruler. This way you will get exact measurements and can be more precise in determining the track's eights. Note in photo 40 that the ruler is placed gently into the track, just touching the track's floor. Using sideheading, you can now read the depth of the track from the horizon to the floor. Then read the measurement to the top of the ridge, peak, or crest. You can now precisely define the proportional size, thus the eights increments, of the pressure release using these measurements.

Also use the ruler to measure the width of the track, using only the true track measurements. Measure the track width from the plate bisecting line to the opposite side of the track. Then measure the plate, the plate-fissure, or the plate-crumble from the wall to the outermost portion of the plate. You now have the exact measurements you need for

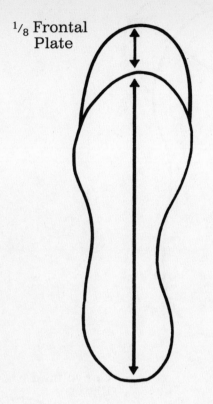

$^1/_8$ Frontal
Plate

71

figuring the proportions and thus to know the eights increments of the plates.

Eventually you will no longer need to use the ruler. After a while, with experience making exact measurements, a simple glance will tell you the eights measurements of any pressure against the wall. There is no need in tracking to be ruler exact. That is, not unless you are involved in a criminal investigation, for which you need precise measurements that will hold up in court. I know from my experience and the experience of countless hundreds of students, that with experience you will be able to just glance at a track and define precisely the eights measurements, without the aid of any measuring device.

To further review and simplify the eights measurements, it is important to remember what pressure against the wall tells you about the track. Pressure against the wall has to do mostly with turning or changing direction and with slowing or stopping. Thus the eights measurements not only define

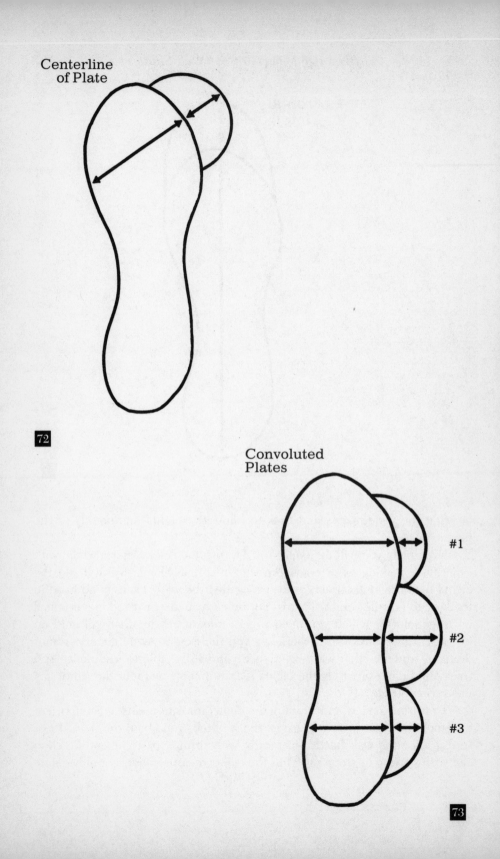

Centerline
of Plate

72

Convoluted
Plates

#1

#2

#3

73

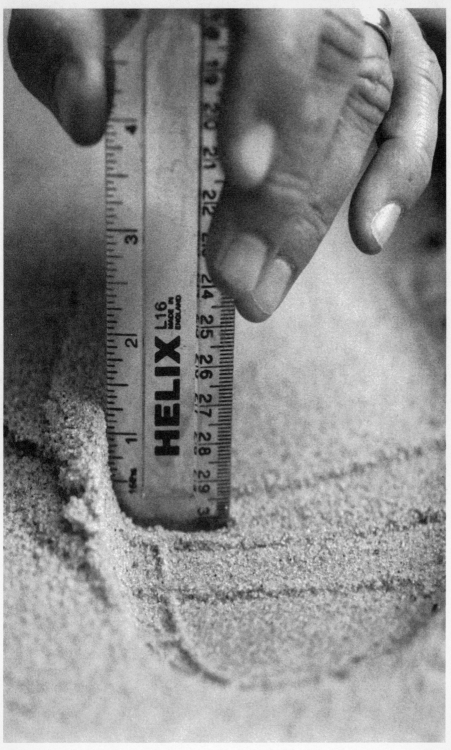

a turn but they tell you exactly how much of a turn or direction change was made. Where before you had the ridge, now you have eight distinct ridges, each with its own gradation of pressure against the wall. Now, instead of just saying that an animal made a slight direction change from 12:00 to 12:15, with the eights gradations you can say that the animal changed direction from 12:00 to 12:11. Add this to the digital pressure releases, which further define a direction change, and you could then know that an animal turned from 12:00 to 12:11 and 16 seconds.

Anytime we break down a pressure release into increments we further define that pressure release and the action that caused it to happen. In essence, what you now have for the pressure against the wall is not just 11 primaries and 11 secondaries, but 1 cliff, 8 ridges, 8 peaks, 8 crests, 1 crest-crumble, 1 cave, 1 cave-in, 8 plates, 8 plate-fissures, 8 plate-crumbles, and 1 explosion. This adds up to 53 pressure releases for pressure against the wall. Remember that they occur again as secondaries, so you can add another 53 secondary pressure releases. Thus you know 106 pressure releases for pressure against the wall. With this expansion of wall pressure releases your track analysis will become even more accurate and definitive.

16. TRACKING AND LAW ENFORCEMENT

I am appalled at how rarely and how ineffectively tracking is used in search and rescue and in general police work, especially since it is the one constant and most obvious evidence we can find. People lost in the wilderness and those engaged in criminal activity must leave tracks, after all; they do not float in and out on the wind. Law enforcement officials today are just not track-conscious to the degree necessary to make it a definitive science. At best, photos or plaster casts are made. Sole patterns are measured and identified as to the manufacturer of the shoe, and from that evidence a guesstimation is made as to size, weight, and height of the wearer. That is where it all ends as far as the criminologists are concerned. Yet, to anyone even mildly trained, this is only the beginning.

As I have come to identify the problem after forty-one years of tracking for the police, officially, unofficially, and undercover, I find that it is not one of incompetence but of lack of education in tracking. Most criminologists and forensic technicians consider tracking to be some sort of romantic art form lost in the mists of time. They see only vague technological applications—not the powerful science it could become with a little education. Thus it has become my lifelong quest to educate the various law enforcement agencies in the science of tracking. Yet despite the thousands of law enforcement officers I have graduated from my school and the countless police classes I have run, I have barely made a scratch on the surface of what needs to be done to make tracking one of the most powerful investigation tools.

Even to this day, with my vast reputation for finding lost people, deciphering crime scenes, and tracking criminals, I am still met with an air of blatant skepticism by most new law enforcement agencies I track for, here and abroad. It isn't until I pull someone from the wilderness, turn up a body, or track down a criminal that they become believers. It's then that I get them to attend my school. After graduation, their arrest record almost always improves exponentially. It is difficult at best to overcome the misconception that tracking is a mythical, ineffective art form and not a science. Though I do admit that we are making some inroads, slowly but effectively.

In the final analysis I believe that all law enforcement agencies should have a trained tracker—someone trained in the science of tracking, as I have been teaching it. It makes no difference if an agency's jurisdiction is at the edge of a wilderness area or in the heart of a city, tracking is a powerful tool. Whether the tracks are found in the soils of a roadless wilderness or on the carpets and floors of our city wilderness, it is still tracking and still powerful evidence. When tracking is finally taken as a serious science, then we will see as many convictions based on the way people walk and the pressure releases they leave as we do based on fingerprint evidence.

No two people walk the same way or leave the same indicator pressure releases. As I explained in chapter 12, indicator pressure releases are pressure releases found every time a foot leaves a print, regardless of whether it's an animal or human doing the walking. In other words, indicator pressure releases are not functional—they have nothing to do with movement, but everything to do with the maker's personal walk. It is the arrangement of these indicator pressure releases that makes each person's, or each animal's, walk different. They are essentially the "fingerprints" of a track and can be regarded in the same way when dealing with identification. In all the countless millions of human tracks I have studied throughout my life I have never seen two people's tracks whose indicator pressure releases are even similar.

When I am called in to investigate a crime scene, the first thing I do is read the overall scenario presented by the tracks. This track scenario tells me exactly what has transpired during the crime. Every action and reaction of the criminal is recorded in each track. Exact physical descriptions can then be identified as well as the time sequence and emotional states. It is much like seeing the whole crime played back. Once I have studied the overall track scenario I then identify the indicator pressure releases and check them against every other track in the pattern. This way I am sure that they are real indicator pressure releases and not just some quirk.

I then set to work preserving the footprint and its indicator pressure releases as evidence. Next to the best track I place a ruler; then I begin taking pictures of the track, using a large-format camera mounted on a tripod. The ruler is important for showing the proper size of the track when it is seen on the photograph. I take several pictures of the track straight down, then at various side angles lit by flash. This way I will have a number of photos and light conditions to choose from. Once the film is developed I enlarge the photos so they show the track at its original size, using the ruler as a reference for that exact size. Once the photo developing is complete and the best photo found I then record the indicator pressure releases.

Covering the photo with a sheet of clear plastic, I draw on the plastic all the indicator pressure releases found in that track. A second sheet of plastic, upon which a foot map grid is measured out and drawn, is then laid over the first. This will give the prosecutors much-needed reference points when the photos are used as evidence. In most criminal cases I make several photos of different left and right tracks, thus showing clearly the redundancy of the indicators. It is always a good idea to have pictures of the suspect's tracks after he has been arrested as a comparison. It is best not to let the suspect know that you are going to photograph his tracks, so he does not deliberately change his walk in an attempt to prevent prosecution.

All of this photographic evidence must be kept as simple and straight-forward as possible. Remember, most law enforcement agencies, prosecutors, lawyers, judges, and juries are not track-conscious. The simpler the better. Be prepared to show in court, especially until the law comes to accept tracking as an exacting science, the differences in pressure releases in two different people. You may have to bring into the courtroom a small tracking box and an overhead projector to show the jury the differences between two walks. The tracking box can also be used to show what pressure releases are and what they mean. This kind of in-court demonstration will enlighten a jury to the power of tracks and thus to the power of your photographic evidence.

With a little tracking knowledge and skill, most law enforcement agents can easily see how the indicator pressure releases can be found in soft soil, but when it comes to forest debris, hard ground, or floors, they are quickly lost. This most certainly need not be the case. Tracks can be seen on every conceivable tracking surface, from deep forest litter, to hard gravel, and even on solid surfaces. However, the trick is to be able to see them, and see them clearly. This is accomplished quite easily once you learn what to look for, how to look, and how to use light to your advantage. Let's now review the two basic techniques for reading tracks on "impossible" surfaces.

Debris Compressions

We discussed debris compressions, and experimenting with reading pressure releases in forest or field litter, in chapter 14. To see debris compressions it is first important to identify the natural loft of the debris, taking in a grander view of the tracking environment. Then, once this natural loft, or debris height, is identified, anything dented into the debris is a track. Once this dent or compression is identified, the tracker can look deeper into the track to isolate broken, abraded, bent, and otherwise disturbed materials to further define the track and subsequently the track pattern. Pressure releases are identified in the same way you learned previously.

Dust and Grit Compressions

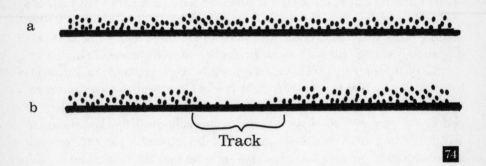

Track

74

Dust and Grit Compressions

This tracking technique, which we also discussed in chapter 14, is the one to use for hard surfaces, such as floors, gravel, and other places like that. In fact, once the technique for reading the dust and grit compressions is mastered, it is used to clarify every other tracking environment. Basically, understanding dust and grit compressions begins with this statement: On every tracking environment there is a collection of dust and grit particles that will be crushed down any time the surface is stepped upon. (See illustrations 74a and 74b). This dust and grit is found on all surfaces from forest debris, to clear tracking soil, to solid surfaces. Whenever a track hits the surface, the dust and grit are crushed down and flattened. Thus a compression.

These dust and grit compressions appear in a very unique way and it is important to identify what the tracker will see. Simply stated, if the overall tracking surface appears shiny, then the track will appear as a dull spot on the surface. Inversely, if the overall tracking surface is dull, then the track will appear as a shiny spot. Fortunately, if throughout the day the tracking surface changes from dull to shiny or from shiny to dull, the tracks will do the opposite. For instance, if you are tracking across the shiny, dew-laden surface of a rock during the morning, the tracks will appear as dull spots. But as the dew dries and the rock surface becomes dull, the tracks become shiny. You are subsequently not lost because of the personality change of any tracking surface.

Before going on to review the exact techniques for reading these dust

Sideheading

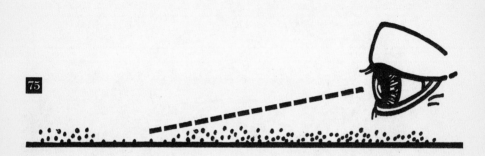

75

and grit compressions, let me first respond to a common question. Many people ask me if dust and grit compressions can still be seen after a heavy rain—after all, they assume, all the dust and grit must be washed away. Not so. Much of the dust can be washed away but not the grit. There is always enough dust and grit after a heavy rain.

Now armed with this information on dust and grit compressions we must learn the techniques for seeing them. Basically there are just two rules you must follow. The first is that you must *look at the track from a severe angle*. The technique is called "sideheading" (see illustration 75 and photo 41). In other words, you would be better able to see a dust and grit compression track twenty feet away from where you stand than by looking straight down at it. To accomplish this severe angle, lie down on the ground and place your cheek to the tracking surface. Closing the upper eye, skim the surface of the ground with your lower eye. This will enable you to see tracks closest to you. Close your lower eye and open your upper eye and you will see the tracks a few feet farther away. To look farther out still, slowly lift your head off the ground.

Sideheading with such severity becomes less necessary after a little practice. Eventually, as your experience with dust and grit compressions grows, you will no longer need to lie on the ground, but will eventually see the tracks from a less severe angle.

The other, more important rule for seeing dust and grit compressions is actually quite simple: *keep the track between you and the source of light*.

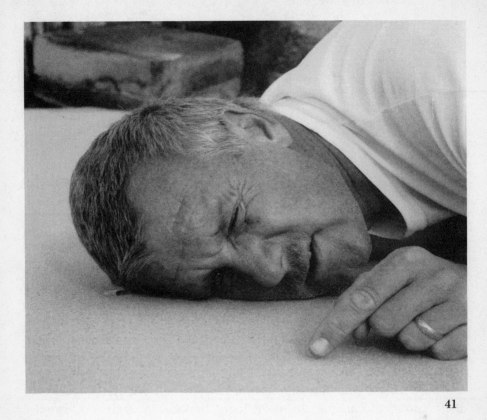

41

You will use this rule not only for the dust and grit compressions but to enhance the tracks in every other tracking environment.

Try this experiment. Wipe a table clean and allow it to stand undisturbed for several hours. Now make several tracks on the table using your hands. Illuminating the table with an overhead light will not show any tracks at all, but moving the light to the opposite end of the table from you will clearly show the tracks. To demonstrate how sensitive this is, find a leaf on untrampled ground. Hold the leaf up to the source of light and view its surface. Now touch your finger lightly to the center of the leaf and hold it back up to the light source again. If the surface of the leaf is shiny, then the print will be dull, and if the surface is dull, your fingerprint will be shiny. Now try this again with a pebble, a stick, a blade of grass, or anything else you can find. The results are equally amazing and simple.

Notice that I say "source of light" rather than identifying that source.

That is because any light will work, be it candlelight, firelight, a flashlight, or sunlight. Of course sunlight will be your primary tracking light. That is why the best time to track is when the sun is at an angle to the ground. Not only does the sun show depth in your tracks through shadow but you can also easily get the track between you and the sun. When the sun is high overhead or when the sky is overcast it is impossible to get the track between you and the light source. However, you can lay a flashlight on the ground or use the palm of your hand to reflect the available light. This is enough to redirect the light so that the track stands out.

The reading of dust and grit compressions will allow anyone to follow and analyze any track across any tracking surface. To the master tracker there is no such thing as the ending of a trail, unless it has been wiped away or destroyed by other tracks or the natural weathering processes. It is my hope that tracking will someday become a valuable tool to law enforcement—as precise and scientific a tool as any other modern investigation technique. But first we must educate the police and then the general public, in much the same way they were educated in fingerprint evidence. I always laugh when I hear of "fiber analysis" evidence used by the FBI. Fiber analysis is like reading fallen redwood trees. They end at fiber analysis, and the master tracker begins with the flatness of dust.

THE FINAL TRACK

As I wrote in my first book, *The Tracker*, "The first track is the end of a string. At the far end, a being is moving; a mystery, dropping a hint about itself every so many feet, telling you more about itself until you can almost see it, even before you come to it." The far end of the string, the last track, the ultimate and final track, can never truly be reached by a tracker. A true tracker is always following a trail, always going from one track to another, from one animal to another, in a neverending cycle.

I used to believe that the skull was the ultimate and final track, but the track goes far beyond the final evidence left on this Earth by man or animal. It reaches far into the world beyond physical life, to that of the vast spiritual domain of the unseen and eternal. It is there too that the tracker must learn to follow the trail, until one day, the ultimate and eternal track allows the tracker to touch God. The final track, the last track, will finally be reached at the feet of the Great Spirit.

At this point in my life, I have been tracking for well over forty years, and I still have not come close to finding the ultimate, final track. A tracker is always tracking, whether in city, suburb, or in the silence of the pathless wilderness. Everything becomes a track and ultimately leads to eternity. We begin tracking as a curious child, touching tracks in wonder. We then begin to pick up that magical string and push ourselves slowly and steadily along the trail. Then we learn the language of pressure releases and are finally able to read the written language of tracks and trails. The very tracks begin to speak to us so that we can see the animal moving within them. Finally, it is not enough to see the animal moving within the tracks. We must become the animal we track, so that we can feel the animal moving within us.

This book then is not only the end but also the beginning. It is the beginning of your "dirt time," and your journey along the trails of life, until you finally become the animal you track. You are also now at the end of the long line of trackers, for truly you are their grandchildren. The information and magic of pressure releases you now possess cannot be learned over a single life span. Instead, it is an accumulation of knowledge that is passed down from generation to generation, with each new generation adding to the whole. Now what follows is for you to master the pressure releases and pass them down to future generations of trackers. As I wrote in the beginning of this book, tracking is a science, an art, and a philosophy, the ultimate extension of awareness. Grandfather considered awareness and tracking to be one and the same, where one could not be complete or exist without the other. The science behind tracking is the pressure releases, the art of tracking is to read the Earth like an open book, and the philosophy of tracking is the deep awareness that it brings—a closer kinship with Earth and Spirit.

Ultimately, the magic of tracking must transcend the limitations of the senses and flesh and reach into the grander domain of the unseen and eternal. It is only when we transcend the flesh, surrender to the Earth and track, that we can ever truly become trackers. I used to watch Grandfather kneel by the first track and bow his head in prayer. At first this struck me as odd, but soon I learned it was as much of tracking as following the tracks. He would pray:

> *"Grandfather, Great Spirit,*
> *Master of all things, you who are called by so many names,*
> *and worshipped in so many ways;*
> *allow me to become the Earth,*
> *teach me to surrender to the tracks,*
> *so that I may become that which I follow,*
> *and if I am worthy,*
> *allow these tracks to lead me closer to You."*

INDEX

Adhesive quality of soil, 156–159
Advanced tracking boxes, 190
Aging characteristics of soil, 165–168, 185
Aging process lesson, 29–32
Animals
  communication with, 34
  and plants, 9
Ant tracking lesson, 21–23
Apache tribe, 3, 26, 33–34
  creation story, 40
  See also Native Americans; Scouts; Stalking Wolf (Grandfather); Tribes
Arrows, 111–112
Art versus science of tracking, 27–32, 201
Assistance digital pressure releases, 108–109
Automobile speedometer, 90, 93
Awareness
  and spirituality, 8, 10–11
  and tracking, 7–11, 13, 22, 170, 191

Blind tracking, 178–180
Bloodhounds, 24
Body functions, 118, 142, 187–190
  See also Pressure release studies, lobular pressure releases
Body posture, 128
Bounding, 80
Brown, Howard (uncle), 1
Brown, Tom, Jr.
  aging process lesson, 29–32
  ant tracking lesson, 21–23
  childhood of, 3, 114
  coaching world-class runners, 89
  grandfather pine lesson, 13–16
  human tracking lesson, 16–18

law enforcement agencies, 201–207
learning tracking, 1, 8–9
meeting Stalking Wolf (Grandfather), 2–3
murder suspect tracking incident, 24–26
nomenclature, 51–53
and Rick (friend), 2–3
shooting of, 26
Show-and-Tell, 2
Tom Brown's Field Guide to Nature Observation and Tracking, 7, 165
tracking cases, 5, 24–26, 33
Brown, Tom, Sr., 1
Building capacity of soil, 164
Bulldozer example, 113

Camouflage, 4
Canopy of treetops, 7
Canvas tracking, 179
Carnivore life, 7
Carpeting, 180
Cave, 59–60, 133, 134
Cave-in, 133–134
Cave-in, cave in, cavein, 60
Changing or maintaining forward motion. *See* Pressure release studies
Checks and balances, 37–38, 113
Claws, 52
Cliff, 54, 131
Colored lights for night tracking, 177
Common tracker, 21
Comparative analysis, 114–115
Concentric rings, 19, 22, 39, 182, 184
Consciousness
  of master tracker, 26
  and the track, 11

211

As you know from reading this book, sharing the wilderness with Tom Brown, Jr., is a unique experience. His books and his world-famous survival school have brought a new vision to thousands. If you would like to go further and discover more, please write for information to:

The Tracker

Tom Brown, Tracker, Inc.
P.O. Box 173
Asbury, N.J. 08802-0173
(908) 479-4681
**Tracking, Nature, Wilderness
Survival School**